All copyrights are retained by the authors.

Cover Art: Rachel Linn

Cover Design: Miranda Schmidt and Nora Broker

Interior Design: Miranda Schmidt

PRINTED IN THE UNITED STATES

Emerge is a publication of Lambda Literary.

Lambda Literary believes Lesbian, Gay, Bisexual, Transgender and Queer literature is fundamental to the preservation of our culture, and that LGBTQ lives are affirmed when our stories are written, published and read.

www.lambdaliterary.org

TABLE OF CONTENTS

Editor's Note

Miranda Schmidt

Introduction

Garth Greenwell

Contents

NONFICTION

PLAYWRITING

POETRY

WRITERS IN RESIDENCE

Acknowledgements

Editor's Note
Miranda Schmidt

When I think of us at the Lambda Writers Retreat for Emerging LGBTQ Voices, I think of the space we created with our writing. Sitting in rows in the main forum at Otis College of Art and Design, every night, we would read from our novels in progress, our fragments of stories, our essays, our poems, our many-voiced plays. For one week, that room was ours. So much greater than the walls that surrounded it, it held a space we wove together with our words, a space we have carried back into our lives outside Lambda, out of that summer and on through the fall and the winter and spring.

I write this from Portland, Oregon, in a neighborhood dotted with queer bars and queer coffee shops and queer clinics. My wife and I live in a life I could not have imagined growing up in the nineties in a conservative Midwestern town in a world that seemed to have no space for queerness at all. When I think of the space of my present life, I still can't help but feel that I'm living inside the impossible. For many of us, especially those of us who grew up with little access to it, queer space can still hold a sense of unreality.

And queer space *is* a little bit magic. It's a shapeshifting creature. It can take many forms: an apartment, a meeting, a bar, a book, a twitter feed, a conversation. Every time queer people gather together, we create new queer space. And in that space create stories, conversations, friendships, futures.

Lambda Literary facilitates the creation of queer spaces for writers and readers. The Retreat, by the very nature of the word, is a space that allows us to step back, momentarily from the rest of the world. Of course, we still bring that world with us. Our writing is full of responses to a world that so often treats us and our spaces with varying degrees of hostility and dehumanization. What struck me most about our writing at Lambda was how beautifully it alchemized anguish, and joy, and honed it into art. In the space of our retreat I watched the words of my fellow fellows blossoming everywhere and this made me feel hopeful about the present and future of queer literature.

When we left Lambda, we stepped off of planes to see headlines of violence, to see the racism of this country writ large and bold and ugly. In these past months, we have seen continued attempts to dehumanize people of color, immigrants, Muslims, women, and, of course, LGBTQ people, and many, many others.

And, in these past months, we have continued to write. We have written to each other on social media and in emails. We have written for publications. We have written for classes. We have written for jobs. We have written for ourselves. We have written poems and essays and stories and novels and plays and cross-genre curiosities. We have written. We continue to write.

I don't know how to live in the moment we're in. But I know writing is my only way forward. Writing is the space that makes a pause for me to think in. It makes room for me to feel in. It allows me a way to respond to the world.

I've had the luck to keep living with the writing in this anthology for these past few months. Editing this anthology, I've gone back, again and again, through the portals of our work, to our nightly readings and the space we created there. I often remember that last night of our retreat, that moment before we stepped back into the world outside, when we danced in the forum and, before I left, I took one last look back.

The chairs are gone, replaced by a circle of bodies and we are all dancing and mingling and swaying and jumping and raising our hands in a space that is ours and a time that is always. Here. Now.

You are holding that space in your hands.

Miranda Schmidt
January 2018

Introduction
Garth Greenwell

In one of my graduate workshops at the University of Iowa, a teacher dismissed my writing about a queer community as "just a sociological report on the behavior of a subculture." This was in 2015, in the rosy light of Obama's second term, just a few months after the Supreme Court declared marriage equality the law of the land—and in one of the country's preeminent creative writing programs, the mere fact of a story taking on queer subject matter meant its expulsion from the world of the literary, its demotion to "a sociological report."

I don't mean to give this moment more weight than it had, and it wasn't representative of my experience in the program at Iowa. But I found myself thinking about it again and again during the week I spent at the Lambda Literary Retreat. I remembered it when a fellow in my workshop marveled that for the first time his work had been discussed without the presence of queerness being the subject of constant scrutiny and debate. I thought of it every time I heard a writer talk about being told—still, now, today—that focusing their work on queer lives would consign them to a "gay ghetto." I thought of it at the end of every workshop session, when I would take stock, amazed, of just how much work you can do in a class, how deep you can get into the real substance of a story, when queer lives don't have to be justified or explained.

I was excited heading into the retreat—I had read my fellows' work and knew how strong it was; I had every reason to expect an excellent workshop. But I had no idea how moved and inspired I would be by the community of queer writers Lambda made possible, or by the rigor and ferocious love my students lavished on one another's work. And the workshop was only part of it. What was thrilling about the retreat was the cross-genre pollination of ideas that happened outside of workshop, the intense, heated, joyful conversations that began at breakfast and continued late into the night.

That heat and intensity and joy reached their peak at the fellows' evening readings, which were less readings than celebrations. Each night I marveled at the range of talent and vision that took the stage, the diverse and daring faces of queer theatre and essay and poetry and fiction; each night I heard brilliant young writers read and perform with such passion and excellence that I literally leapt to my feet. This anthology lets you experience that excellence for yourself. Pay attention: these are writers that you'll be reading for the rest of your life.

Garth Greenwell
January 2018

FICTION

Song, Silence, Pain
an excerpt
Nawaaz Ahmed

The imam speaks: How magnificent the universe is, my brothers and sisters. So vast that no human being can take full measure of its vastness, so beautiful that no human eye can perceive its every beauty, so mysterious that no human mind can comprehend all its mysteries. Yet every part of the universe—from a massive galaxy to a minute whirling electron—follows every law that has been prescribed for it by the creator, Allah, the Exalted in Might, the All-Knowing. Every part of the universe submits to the will of Allah, which is the essence of Islam, and thus every part of the universe is Muslim. The stars are Muslim, the sun is Muslim, the moon is Muslim. Doesn't the Quran say, 'The sun runs his course for a period determined for him: that is Our decree. And the moon—We have measured for it mansions to traverse till it returns to its withered state, like a stalk of date. It is not permitted for the sun to catch up to the moon: each swims along in its own orbit according to Our law'?

And here on earth, every mountain is Muslim, every ocean is Muslim, every river is Muslim: they all follow the natural laws that have been laid down for them. Every animal is Muslim, every tree is Muslim, every bird is Muslim: from birth to death every organ, every tissue, every cell in their bodies follows the laws that have been designed uniquely for them. Can the nightingale sing any other song than has been ordained for it? Every note that it sings has been written for it. It can no more change its song than it can shed its wings.

*

The doctor speaks: Why poetry? We may as well ask: why life?

We cannot apprehend the one without the other: to read or write poetry is to explore the complexity of life, to live is to experience the arresting reality of poetry. If life is a picture then poetry is the faint flickering light that illuminates it. If life is a lamp then the stirring overlapping shadows it casts all around us are poems.

And the poet is life's prophet. Look around you: we are in an auditorium, but we're also in a city, in a country, in a continent, on a planet, in a solar system, in a galaxy, in a universe that is so vast that we can scarcely imagine its limits. Yes, science can provide us with more and more information, more and more details. But who is to weave all this information and all these details together into a tapestry that we can grasp, when our minds are small and evolved to focus mainly on the here and now: Why is my leg itching? What's cooking for dinner tonight? When will this loudmouth stop babbling?

*

His daughter speaks: Father, you taught us to look beyond subsistence, beyond what is needed to keep mind and body together. You taught us to probe the universe for hidden truth and beauty, to seek sustenance only in the true and the truly beautiful. You taught us to question everything else—rituals, tradition, faith, ties. You taught us to embrace everything that life challenged us with: you said that it's precisely there, in these moments, that true poetry resides.

You taught us to love: to love those discoveries that brought us unexpected joy, to love those moments that pressed us to the brink of new discoveries, to love those beings who made each moment burn and crackle with the promise of illumination. I love someone like that. She's beautiful, she's wise, she's brave, she's strong. In her presence the universe reveals its hidden beauty; in her presence the universe shines with a new light. Isn't someone like that worthy of love? Isn't love like that worthy of our deepest gratitude?

Ahmed

*

The universe speaks: Moon, you were waiting there for us that night. Round, full of yourself, drunk on that treacherous moonshine that promises invincibility, the certainty that everything can be overcome, that nothing leaves a mark. Love, hate, desire; birth, death, despair. Ecstasy, misery. Song, silence, pain. Everything can be defied, nothing is sacred. We need only choose which gods we worship, which rituals serve our days—

And we believed you. Fools that we are, we wanted to believe. Tomorrow, you will be there again, waiting for us—diminished.

Nawaaz Ahmed is a transplant from Tamil Nadu, India. He holds an MFA from the University of Michigan, Ann Arbor, and has been awarded residencies at Yaddo, Macdowell, and the Virginia Center for the Creative Arts. He's a Breadloaf waiter and a Kundiman fellow. He lives in Brooklyn, working on his first novel "Sings Like A Bird," which this selection is excerpted from.

The Book of Fish
an excerpt
Callum Angus

In a food coma later that night, I stare at the local news on mute, one of three channels that reach me in my little beige box of a room. On screen, sirens flash noiselessly; police usher a group of people—enough for a high school band—out the back of an 18-wheeler on the side of a darkened highway; German shepherds bark at their heels without sound; the final image is that of a nondescript bureaucratic building, which if you look closely is fringed by curlicues of barbed wire along its high, pastel walls.

Emilio was a little girl the first time he crossed the line. He remembered sitting patiently on the bus, hands folded in his lap while the border guards disemboweled his mother's suitcase. They stayed with an uncle sweating motor oil in San Antonio. One afternoon Emilio snuck behind his shop to where a pit bull had just given birth to a litter. He took off his Mary Janes to feel the warm squish of afterbirth between his toes.

The second time he crossed he was in between boy/girl/child. As soon as his mother's silhouette disappeared from view he ducked into a bodega bathroom and chopped off his hair with a pair of kitchen shears. With a student visa and a plane ticket he left Mexico behind for Massachusetts. He noticed the sideways glances and sniggers from the agents watching his gym sock package on the body scan, but he ignored them and they, in a rare display of restraint, ignored him back.

The third time Emilio crossed the line it was against his will while a man with a CB radio like a bloated tick at his lapel barked out orders. Emilio stared at the floor mottled pink like canned meat. The officer pulled him up by the collar. Emilio kept his eyes down, no Hail Marys for him now, just the Questions: *Where'd your prick go, little man? You got no dick? The fuck we gonna do with no-dick? A girl thinks she's somebody's nephew in San Antonio. Gimme a break. Put him—her—back in the pen with the others. It's lunch time.* Inside the women's detention center he is watched, he becomes everything that watching means. 177 sets of eyes follow him around. The moms are scared without their daughters, and motherless daughters are nice to him with no parents around. Had he been there longer he might have made friends. But he spoke English and so they fast-tracked him back to Mexico to keep him from letting the others know the meaning of *habeas corpus* and illegal detention. Even so, he bleeds from weeks without his hormones, too shy to ask for a tampon from the women around him, but still growing facial hair because that never stops. The bearded lady, the bleeding man.

The fourth time, the last time, was quieter. No diesel buses, no hypertensive guards. Emilio walked in silent single file behind strangers in the dark. Chilly points of stars spatter across the big night. They don't deviate from the forced march of their guide—a large silent man who carries a pistol in a holster under his armpit. *For coyotes*, he says. Each day he looked at Emilio a little closer and Emilio pretends his jawline isn't falling away from lack of testosterone, that his love handles aren't returning, that he isn't slowly changing like the schools of native fish in the Nueces, hybridizing into some new species in a process parallel to aging. On the third night, the guide approached him.

"Who do you think you're fooling? Maybe for the first day or two, but you thought I wouldn't notice?"

"I paid you already. Leave me alone." Emilio, perfectly aware at how easily a face can waver between dandy and drag, straining to feel the magnetism of an invisible borderline.

"So testy. You can't hide grapefruits like that from a conocedor." In the dark Emilio knows the hand is there before he feels it brush the hem of his shirt. Fingertips skim his unbound chest, binder earlier abandoned in favor of baggy shirts and lung room. He knocks the hand away.

"You do your job and I'll do mine." Emilio says.

"What's your job, freak?"

"You get me back to the states; I walk, and look good doing it."

Cursing him, the guide stalks off. Emilio exhales in shaky re-lief. Without explanation the guide kicks at his flock, rousing them and force-marching all night until the morning begins to bloody the sky. The guide shoves Emilio forward off in a direction away from the group, point-ing for him to keep walking. The others continue on with the man until he delivers them into the waiting embrace of meat packing plants and rich white families in need of nannies. Emilio doesn't stop until he reaches the wheat fields of West Texas.

Callum Angus holds an MFA in fiction from the University of Massachusetts Amherst, and his stories and essays have appeared in The Common, The Offing, The Normal School, BuzzFeed, The Millions, Queen Mob's Tea House and Rain Taxi. He teaches writing at Smith College.

Milo
Quentin Greif

When I was fourteen my dad's best friend gave me $400 to jerk off in front of him. I remember staring into his eyes, as he stroked himself too, the money already stowed away in the pocket of my jeans, thinking about the Diesel bomber jacket I was going to buy in an hour. Later at the mall, wearing the jacket, I told Alex the story. Her eyes widened and we both began to laugh. *What a fucking idiot*, was all she could say, tears streaming down her face.

I did it once a week for an entire year until he finally said it made him feel too guilty. By then he'd taught me enough though, and there were others, other dumb mother-fuckers with cash they obviously didn't need.

*

I drive up 281, the neon blurs beside me through the window, reflecting off the lingering droplets of water from the rain earlier in the day. My windows are down. Breeze blows on me like breath. When I drive I feel alive; the car moves when I want it to, every vibration running through my body.

San Antonio is unseasonably cool tonight. I hit the loop at seventy-five miles an hour, passing straight under it toward the outer suburbs. They rise up on the hills beside me, the same home duplicated a thousand times. I once lived there, before my fucking dad walked out and my mom lost it. Now she sits on the couch, wrapped in a snuggie I bought her off an infomercial, taking a clonazepam every couple of hours.

Past the suburbs the hills are dotted with trees. You could drive for hours and it would just be the hills, up and down like the slowest roller-coaster you've ever been on. I turn onto a small county road toward Alex's house. We work in tandem with each other. Tonight I need her to be my watcher as I've dozens of times for her. It is how we make sure the other is safe when we're with clients. It's easy for us. We mostly use craigslist:

looking for generous men. And besides that we both have our regulars.

Alex's parents are never home. She once referred to them as "freelance doctors." They must be shitty doctors, because they don't ever send her enough money. We like it though, the fucking around with men. It's so easy. Half the time they only want to watch you get yourself off. Alex once made three grand in a single session just so the guy could film her and another girl eating each other out. It pays to be underage I guess; they get off on that. So I keep everything smooth, shaved, and waxed. It's gotten a little harder lately, but I can still look like a kid when I know that's what they want.

I pull onto her graveled driveway. Trees scrape the sides of the car like fingernails. Her house emerges out of the night like some sort of apparition. I love her house. Whenever I can, I spend nights there. It is our sanctuary, and we never bring men back to this house. In the front there is a huge porch that wraps all the way around to the back on both stories.

I get out of the car and walk around to the back and knock on the glass door. I can see Alex walking down the stairs barefoot, wearing a black tank-top and a short black skirt. She has a kind of a goth look the guys seem to dig, so we play it up whenever we're taking pictures of her.

Watsup Milo. She's leaning against the door now, staring lazily in my direction.

I have a date, need a watch, you game?

She laughs at this, steps out onto the porch and grabs a pack of cigarettes sitting on one of the tiny decorative tables.

Why are you laughing?

Cause I thought you were going to plan this shit better. You show up here and its already fucking late, I wanted to smoke a joint and go to bed early, maybe actually go to school tomorrow.

Awww come on baby don't be mad. I wrap my arms around her waist and rest my head on her shoulder.

She pushes me away. *Fucking sleaze Milo that's what you are.* She's smiling a little though, I can tell she's not really mad, but she still isn't really looking at me either.

What's wrong baby? What happened? Tell me.

Don't coo at me with that baby voice. It doesn't do shit for me. Turns me off actually, straight dries me up.

Fine. Be that way, I say with finality.

I grab a cigarette off the table, surprised the porch had managed to keep them dry, leaky as it is. Or maybe she'd been sitting out here all afternoon smoking, after the rain stopped. I look at her looking out at the dead grass of the yard that ends abruptly forty feet away in a thick clump of trees. Her family's property goes back for five acres. It was given to her mama by her grandpa who bought it after years of hard work. Before that her mom's family was from Mexico. We drove there once, together, to Monterrey. From San Antonio down it feels like one seamless place with a giant scar along the Rio Grande for no good reason.

Talk to me. I'm still looking at her.

She called today.

What'd she want? Money?

Yeah of course. She asked how mom and dad were and I had to tell her fuck if I know.

We were silent again for a couple of minutes. Whenever her sister called she got like this. Andrea had run off a few years back after getting out of Laurel Ridge, the all-in-one service center for all the crazies of north San Antonio. Half our school went there to pick up their Adderall or Ritalin or Wellbutrin or whatever-the-fuck their "needed" prescriptions were, but Andrea had been for real committed. That was something different. Put Alex through hell, because she was the one mostly dealing with it. When they let her out she turned eighteen a month later and just left. Now she periodically called, asking for money, "checking in" on Alex, but I knew Andrea and she was the one who needed checking in on.

I'm sorry Alex, I say quietly.

What for? It's not your fault her mind's so fucked.

I know but still.

Anyway what's the play tonight?

You'll do it then?

Yeah of course, but you owe me one, and start fucking planning better. She turned and blew a thick plume of smoke in my direction, like a dragon, sexy almost.

I dropped my phone again it's all busted, but I think I can get a new one after tonight! It's a Fred France night.

Oh lord, she says and laughs again, this time with less of a sharp edge, although her laugh always has a little cut to it, which breaks my heart every time.

Fred France is the father of Logan France, probably the worst girl to ever walk the halls at Ronald Reagan High-School, and that's saying a lot. As if that school wasn't bad enough already Logan France has to smear her bad attitude around like she's some sort of fucking queen, all because her dad owns some car dealerships. Back when our families actually went to church we used to see the France family always sitting in the front pew, all three of them with that shining blonde hair. Logan was the only kid they ever had so they spoiled that bitch. Daddy France and I started up when I met him one night at a bar way on the edge of town called the Office Lounge. It was a weeknight, so not many people were there, but he was sitting toward the end of the bar. I'd driven out there to meet a client that never showed and before long old Fred was buying me shots of whiskey. He took me back to his place and gave me five hundred dollars to sit on his face while he jacked off then asked me to cum on him. The next Monday at school Logan was bragging about how her daddy had sent her and her mama on a trip to New York to buy her a homecoming dress and I just kept replaying Fred's cum-soaked face in my head. I'd seen him a few times since. One time he wanted me and another boy to mess around in front of him. Another time he wanted to just watch me play with myself. He has a purple dildo that is almost comically huge. I wonder how he hides that from his wife.

Let's get going then I'll follow you in the truck, Alex says, stubbing out the cigarette.

I walk around to the front and get into my car. Alex pulls the truck up behind me and her front lights shine through my back window like two piercing eyes. We drive out onto the country road toward the bar I'm supposed to meet Fred at. Alex will hang back a bit and wait until Fred's car leaves the lot, I'll be in it at that point, then she'll follow us to his house and wait at the end of the long driveway. If I screamed she'd be able to hear me. Shit happens sometimes when you do this, but the other is always close by. Some of these pricks don't have any respect, but I guess that's what you can expect from a bunch of child-fuckers.

The landscape grows wild around us. Trees on either side are so close together they look like giant stone walls rising. I think I can see more stars as we drive. The road is shitty out here and my car begins to bump along; occasionally a big enough dip causes the front fender to scrape the black tar. Alex follows about a half a mile back, but I can still see her lights in the rearview. It's going to be about twenty minutes until we reach the bar so I push in the car lighter and inhale a big breath of Marlboro smoke. It excites me, the nicotine coursing through my lungs, the cool wind on my face, another adventure with Alex and money at the end of it all. My mind returns to Alex getting dressed. I see her face in the mirror, strange and beautiful. She wishes we could do this forever, that we wouldn't grow old. I would follow her anywhere. I never want us to part.

I pull into the dingy parking lot. Alex waits up the road, but I can feel her presence through the trees. I walk inside and Fred is at the end of the bar. I notice his face is flushed and I immediately know he is pretty drunk. This might not take as long as I thought. Maybe Alex and I will be smoking that joint in an hour flat in her bedroom. I walk over to him and sit next to him. It's important to never talk first, they get testy that way, see you as pushy, so I wait for him to say something. The bartender walks over. I can see in his eyes he's going to kick me out, but then he looks at me and Fred together and gets the play. *What'd'ya want?* he asks gruffly.

Three shots of whiskey and a beer, I don't care which, Fred says.

He comes back over and lines up three glasses in front of me and pours the amber liquid over them. I take them back with a sip of beer in between each one. Fred drops two twenties and gets up to leave. I follow.

Outside the night is still. I do not see Alex, but I feel her close and

I know she feels me too. We have talked about this often: the instinctual magic that we are bonded by, how we know when the other is in harm's way. Fred is staggering a little toward his truck. He is drunk and for a moment I wonder if he is going to ignore me altogether. It happens: men having a sudden last minute change of heart. Or perhaps he just wants something in the car, something quick. He's never touched me before, but I prefer that to going back to his house. He turns.

I want to fuck you tonight, he says the way I imagine he opens a discussion for a new business venture of his.

Only a few times had men wanted that, but I'm not going to hesitate at all. He's drunk, he wants something new, this could be a windfall.

Five-hundred, and you wear a condom.

He opens his wallet and peels off six hundred dollar bills and slides them into the back pocket of my jeans cupping my ass. *No condom,* he whispers. I can smell liquor on his breath, damp and sour, but for a few seconds I am almost excited. I like him in control.

From this point forward only sir or daddy comes out of your mouth when you refer to me.

Yes sir.

He climbs into the driver's seat and I climb into the passenger seat. We pull out of the parking lot and I glimpse Alex's lights in the mirror, a quick flash of comfort, before I notice Fred unzipping his pants. He cups his hand to the back of my head, one hand on the wheel, and guides my head down to his crotch. We have a while ahead of us, and I move slowly. Eventually, he starts to press harder on the back of my head, I choke and I can tell he likes that. Suck it bitch, I hear above me and for a minute I can't breathe. He releases me all at once though, he doesn't want to cum in the car, and I thrust back and rest my head on the seat. I feel drunk now, blood is pumping in my ears. I light a cigarette without asking and he looks over, but doesn't say anything as I roll down the window and blow the smoke out. I have a second to check the passenger side mirror, and she's still there following me. She is restless, perhaps bored, but I know she is razor sharp in her focus. We both know how to follow just the right distance back, to look out for any signs of danger.

I feel bold tonight, almost idiotically so, and I turn to look at him, a pathetic fucking slump in his seat. Anger suddenly wells up in me that I cannot identify, I feel the blood rushing faster through my veins. So many thoughts push into my mind all at once, as if all the darkness of my life has decided to flood into my head at just this moment. I've felt this before, this rage, and something about him sitting there ignites it. I want to hurt Fred.

So where's Logan this weekend, I say casually, like it's nothing, like we chat about her all the time. He looks over at me like I'm something different, something he cannot control.

Keep her fucking name out of your mouth.

She know you like to get your dick sucked by little boys, to fuck them in the ass, I say it quickly and begin to laugh, but before I can even reach the cigarette back up to my lips I feel his balled fist slam into the side of my face. My vision goes out, black and I hear a ringing in my ear. He keeps punching and my head flings out the window a little. Then I feel him grip my throat with one hand, hard, like he's going to kill me. It all begins to go black when I hear the screeching of tires and a loud thump at the front of the car. I am pushed forward by the force of the sudden stop and my forehead slams into the dashboard.

Fuck, he is saying and I hear a door slam. Everything is moving, but one thought overtakes me: get the fuck out of the car. I open the door and fall four feet to the ground.

What the fuck are you doing, I hear distantly and I know it's only seconds before he's going to come back around. He reaches me and I feel one solid kick in my ribs and then a loud crack. Fred screams and I hear him fall beside me. Alex is next to me in a rush, like an animal ready to attack and I see her on the ground with her gun at Fred's temple.

Get the gun out of his glove compartment Milo, now, I take a moment to register the words, but I scramble up and open the compartment and reach in and grab the smooth nozzle, lighter than I expected. I run my thumb quickly to the handle and grab hold of it and bring it out of the car.

Did you hit him? Is he going to die? I hear my voice crack, I'm not sure why exactly I'm crying.

No, but I fucking tried. Now you listen to me you piece of shit pervert. You're going to drive home and none of this shit ever happened. You fucking understand.

I understand you fucking cunt, he spits out and Alex brings the butt of the gun down across his face.

I'm sorry I didn't hear you. We good here, or you want him to call the cops and say you raped him.

Yes, we're good, he gasps out holding his nose now as it bleeds. He gets up, slams the passenger door, stumbles to the front, and drives off.

I suddenly realize how quickly I'm breathing, the gun is sweaty in my hand, when I hear a sound I hope I never hear again. A buck is moaning in the grass about five feet from us, hit by the car while Fred was beating me. Alex walks toward it and looks down for a few seconds. She looks back at me, then raises the gun to kill it.

Wait.

We have to kill it Milo.

Just wait.

I walk forward and look down at it too. Then I raise my gun, discharge the weapon and watch the bucks head burst open. For a few minutes we stand in the complete silence of the nothingness, watching dark liquid leak out of the hole in the animal's head.

We stay quiet on the drive home. I can't focus on anything, the world in front of me seems to fade in and out in waves. Next thing I know; Alex is helping me up the creaky wooden stairs to her room. In the bathroom she undresses me like a child and turns on the shower. I step in and the hot water stings against my face. My whole body aches. She comes back in and I step out of the shower. She dries me off and puts sweats on me. I comply with how she needs me to move.

We walk back into the room and she goes to her drawer. She struggles with a pill bottle cap then pours four blue saucers into her hand. I take two and she knocks back the others and we slide into bed together. Tenderly we fold into each other, wrapping our legs together like tentacles. I smell her, a scent I recognize as if it were my own, and I drift into blackness.

When I wake she is standing by the window. It is dark, I don't know how much time has passed. She is smoking a joint and looking up at the moon. I watch her from the bed, unable to move. I realize I would kill for her, something she already knew she would and could do for me. She turns as I inhale, her eyes glinting in the soft light. *I know you*, I whisper softly. She looks a second longer, she doesn't need to respond, and turns back toward the window.

Quentin Greif is a writer living in Hoboken, New Jersey.

Give Us What We Want
Matthew R.K. Haynes

John John pointed from the Kona coast out to the sea just as he was going to say something important, something I thought was going to be *brah, brah, let's fucking leave this place, go the mainland, shak in Florida, just you and me.* Instead he said, *what the fuck*—something caught his attention out there. I couldn't look because I was focused on his neck muscle, so tight it was a like a rib. Then he stood up and said, *fuck, what you think,* and looked down at me sitting on the bleached log, my feet dug into the sand, a dented beer can clutched in my left hand. He was blocking the sun, so when I looked up his whole body was dark except for light at the edges, cutting between his curly, brown hair—like is this what people saw when they were out in the desert and Jesus gave them water and shit?

Ho, you da kine? he asked. But I hadn't smoked in a while because it confused me for days, like I couldn't think right, or couldn't find my thoughts, and I felt like those were the only things that belonged to me.

I was living with my Auntie K because mom odeed on junk and was taken to Kahi Mohala on Oahu, and dad just packed up and cut while I was with mom in the hospital. And he took it all, like even my socks and drawings of Hawaiian birds I did in 8th grade that were pinned to the wall. I spent whole days sitting in my empty room wondering why.

What'd you see? I asked. John John spun around and pointed. The water was calm and a mile out I saw a dark speck bobbing, the raise of arms taking long strokes.

Stupid fucka's out there, he said and I nodded, denting the beer can a bit more, dreaming that the guy was heading to New Zealand or Australia, and wishing that it was me and John John, that we had those kinds of balls.

Hope he makes it, I said.

He won't, John John said. *Shark meat.* Then he walked up the shore to a plastic grocery bag filled with fridge ice and beer. His shorts had loosened enough that a tan line showed, and that reminded me of how many long, mostly empty days we'd spent outside together. John John was graduated, but I dropped out when it all went down with mom. He was my second cousin and also lived with Auntie K. We talked it out one night about how he was the son of Tommy and Leilani, and Leilani was the daughter of Ilima, my mom's older sister. Tommy cut town when Leilani was arrested for plotting to bomb the Royal Hawaiian, got herself all caught up in the sovereignty movement. Ilima was in Florida and there was no money to get John John over there. We'd both been with Auntie K for six months, John John just a couple weeks ahead of me, and I had this feeling like Florida was never going to happen for him. So, when Auntie K didn't have us picking up dog shit or feeding the chickens or spraying the lines to keep out the roaches and centipedes, we were at the beach, and as often as we could, we were drinking. Being outside so much kept us dark. The only difference was John John had been raised going to the gym and had a thick, beefy look to him. The combination of all that was too much to handle some days, and I thought that maybe this day I was going to break and hug him too long or kiss him or try and hold his hand. And when I was all spacey from the paka, I let myself think he'd be fine with all that.

Tommy called again, John John said, chugged the rest of his beer and returned to the bag for another. *You like?* he asked.

Shoots, I said and he tossed one.

Fucka said was going take one more month. He cracked his beer and chugged that one then crushed and pitched it into the surf. *You gotta get out too, boy.* The statement seemed so distant. John John had said this shit before, but it was never, *boy, you gotta come with me to Florida,* which made me think that he was trying to make a break, a clean break, that maybe when he got to Florida he'd even ditch Tommy and change his name and cut his hair and stop drinking and get a real kine job and disappear into it all. Maybe that was the only way to get reborn.

Not sure if I want to, I said.

There's nothing here, brah.

I told John John that everything was here—what was left of family and the ocean, and that was all we needed. Once I said it, I knew it wasn't true. He had no family worth anything to him—Auntie K was just a place to crash—and the ocean was just a barrier between him and all the possibilties. We were not standing on the same land. I stared at him, hoping he'd get that I was saying *me*—I was still here.

John John snatched the last two beers from the bag and threw me one. He walked to the water, letting the small tides wash up to his calves then continued walking to an outcrop of rocks. Now that he'd gone, I noticed the day was hot and I tried to ease back into the sun a bit.

John John and I shared a room and there were nights when he'd read to me from *Heads by Harry* cause it all takes place on the Big Island, and we'd talk about how we should write about *our* lives and all the shit that'd *we'd* gone through. Sometimes, when the occasional rains would come and we stayed indoors, we'd sit in the bedroom and I'd draw pictures of John John on lined paper. He'd do the David pose and the Thinker pose or like he was throwing a spear. I wasn't sure if I wanted to be with John John or just didn't want him to go, like if I was going to be stuck here, because I felt like I had to be, then I didn't want to go it alone.

Eh, hele mai, John John called from the rocks, waving his right hand to come.

I didn't want to fucking look at some seashell and I didn't care if he found another shark tooth, and I was feeling pretty buzzed. I stood up and looked over.

Brah? he said, maybe shocked that I hadn't come running. So, I slowly walked over, along the wet sand. The bit of cool felt good.

No need hurry, he said, his hands on his hips.

John John grabbed my arm when I was close enough and pulled me to a small crater in the outcrop. In the bowl was a green sea turtle, the size of a family wok, that must have come in on a wave and gotten stuck.

It was waiting for the water to come again and catch its ride home. We couldn't be sure how long it had sat there, but we'd been at the beach since ten and it was way past noon. It could have been there over night.

Shit, brah, I said. *Fucka's gotta weigh a hundred pounds. Help me get it in the wada.*

Naa, John John said, then he looked out to the ocean, squinting, maybe looking for that swimmer, maybe thinking about where he was going, or maybe thinking about where he was coming from. *You sacrifice one honu, you get one wish,* he said.

One night when mom was high on junk she told me that when she was a little girl, her dad and uncles took her to a certain beach during the night and hunted honu to make turtle soup. She said they'd straddle its back, pinning the flippers with their knees, grab right under their chins, pull back and slit their throats. Then she said, her eyes red and gooey, *you know, boy, the buggas cry.* I knew I never wanted to see a turtle cry.

John John, brah, those are just stories, I said. *Come on, help me.*

I reached down and put my hands under one side. The belly of the shell was tacky, so it must have been there for a while. The turtle didn't even try to pull its head in. John John bent down and moved in close, putting his hands on my shoulders. His eyes were red and gooey too, but for different reasons. *Brah, maybe our wishes come true,* he said.

It seemed like a whole day went by, or a whole summer, as we stayed just like that, silent and steady. I can't say if it was his hands on me or his eyes on me or how I somehow saw the future where John John kept drinking and started in on Ice, like his old man, and turned wholly bad, or the idea of my wishes coming true, but I broke the stillness with the nod of my head.

John John wandered off digging through the bushes and under Kiawe trees. I went back to the bleached log where I'd left my beer, drank and filled it with sea water to wet the turtle. Its fins moved and it looked relieved, and that made me feel so fucking bad, so much that I wished I hadn't given it any water at all. When I saw John John walking back, I almost said *No, brah, no.* But I felt like I had to follow through with the decision I made, like all the men in our families had done all their lives.

John John had a sharp piece of lava that had probably been used for digging into coconut, and that's how I tried to think of it—this is like digging into a coconut. He straddled its shell and grabbed its head. I thought it might try to snap—I wanted it to snap.

E ha'awi ia makou I ka makou makemake, John John said, his bass voice booming. Then he jammed the rock into its throat. The turtle jolted and its flippers trembled, and it hissed. So, John John kept stabbing until there was plenty blood, until it stopped shaking, until all we heard was its heavy breathing, and then nothing at all. I had closed my eyes for a while instead of looking away, the sound of John John, and all those words, still echoing. When I opened, I saw strange thick tears from pearly black eyes.

I wanted a sign. I waited for the sky to go dark and rumble or the ocean to rise or Mauna Loa to blow its top, but nothing.

John John fingered some of the blood and put a stripe down my forehead to the bridge of my nose, then a stripe across his own. We sat there like that, and suddenly I was scared. More scared than when Mom tripped and when Dad flew. Because, what if our wishing two separate things cancelled the other out? What would we be left with, but a dead turtle between us?

Matthew's new multi-genre collection, "Distant Tides", has been chosen for the Wayne Westlake Monograph Series and is forthcoming from Kuleana Press-University of Hawai'I, Manoa. "Give Us What We Want" is from his new short story collection, "Blue Hawai'i".

Feed Them
an excerpt
Ammi Keller

A straight girl came to the land, a hobo with her two queer friends, just after she'd run out of psych meds. Her hair was such a tangle, folded High Life caps crushed around the dreads. She was young and feminine in a way that made my clit prickle, with jealously maybe, and she asked all the wrong questions around the fire.

"What were you like before?"

I was normal enough, I said. I was a punk and a bisexual (we didn't have queer yet, I told her) but I was spoiled, by which I meant firmly middle class. My mother was a high school science teacher, my dad a chemist who worked on food—tweaking red dye number nine, making Doritos smell like jalapenos.

So yes I dropped out of high school, but I wasn't alone—there was this tiny surge of us vegan, anti-authoritarian, letter writing youth. The intimation was that I'd get my GED and go back to college, and get more out of it later; my parents had faith. Then suddenly I was twenty-five. I was living in New Orleans. I'd seen a woman who'd been raped dumped out of the side of a car onto the steps of our squat.

The girl slugged down more Wild Irish Rose instead of sharing her own story. Since we weren't making homebrew yet, she was the only one, and what I should have seen as her burden I saw as my problem. A few minutes later she teased someone by asking for their "real name" and I sent her to bed, cruelly, like a grandmother. She was only twenty years old.

And in the morning her friends found her dead in her one person REI tent. It might have been shroudlike if it wasn't bright blue. They had to pull her out by her feet in her darned wool socks, revealing next her stripped wool tights, like a mystery, thinking they could still revive her. Pulling on her so that her lowest ribs were revealed where her shirt rode up, the pale skin between her bones patterned with dirt like paper over which charcoal had been rubbed. We realized she'd eaten a year's supply of pain pills out of the apothecary—an irrecoverable loss—but how can you be angry at someone in that much distress? I'm not sure what I would have done with my feelings in the abstract, back in the "real world." But here there was a body to deal with, one that was stiffening into rigor mortis. I closed her eyes because, in a group, I am the person most likely to reach forward. The coldness of her eyelids, hard to pull like window blinds so that for a split second I did need to think about the mechanics, travelled after up my arm into my neck, my teeth. I realized we'd have to move her, this block of wood in the shape of a child.

Kaden said the rigor would wear off. It was early spring and still cold but the body already smelled faintly, that sweet smell, almost gentle, almost like cunt, that weighs down the air. Kaden said now was the best time to move her and when the board of her went up I knew I was no longer a child, no longer a woman, no longer a citizen. I could not believe flesh could get that hard. We aren't anybody, I told Mike, and they hide it from us. We're just stones made out of universe.

Ammi Keller's work appears in The Best American Nonrequired Reading 2015 She is at work on a novel-in-stories about Hurricane Katrina, sexuality and disaster capitalism.

Sanctuary City
an excerpt
Tanea Lunsford Lynx

Fire. That animal thing. That untamable ruinous thing. That does—that can engulf your life in a fan of flame. Suffocate it and make it look beautiful to you. Hold you by the neck and change your scent. Make all of the things you've ever owned one charred color and one charred smell.

My mother has set many fires.

Years before she smelled the top of my head as a child and knew I would love her back she walked to the store on an errand and saw a dead vine whoring tangled in the uniformed existence of a fence. And she set the fire as she walked.

Flour. Milk. A head of cabbage.

She walked the route back and the entire fence was aflame like a bible story. She hurried home.

My mother says I've always smelt this way. The top of my head has always warned her like the smell of something on-fire. The smell that says something is happening. Something needs your attention. Something is moving toward you becoming real, maybe in front of your face. Maybe she manifested me before I was born. Maybe I was there. I can see her lighting that fence on fire when I hear her talk.

Fire—

Is nothing sacred to you? Is no thing sacred to you? Where do you draw the line? Is every *thing* fair game?

Ruthless fire wants the house and the keys, it says: "Let me hold on to that metal until its naught/not/knot."

In our ghettoes, children light their beds on fire when their mothers are evicted.

Do you ever look at your house and wonder what of it you would save? Fire licks both palms and spreads more. Wants everything until there is nothing. Always. No one wishes fire on anyone else lightly.

Fire is getting you now. It knows the bad things you said. At least it acts that way. Like it knows all of the bad things all of your ancestors have ever said or thought. It acts as the sole victim to each of these crimes, ever. And it remembers. It makes you remember too. Wring out all of your guts trying to remember. It gets its revenge. If it hasn't yet then you'd better enjoy the civil enemies you have left.

Fire. That hot thing that ruins your family and makes you wet your bed when it flames your dreams unquenched at night. It threatens again and again to ruin you. And ruin you more. And ruin you better.

She didn't mean for us to be there. She didn't know we'd be there. After my mother set fire to our house I started wetting the bed again. I convinced Malik that it was him. After a while he'd been so careful to not drink anything after dinner and pee before bed and soon we'd all known it was me.

When we went to visit my mother in the hospital she was wearing all white like an angel. She had called us at my grandmother's house beforehand to tell us to bring her a twopiece with a biscuit from *Popeye's* from the storefront on Geneva and Mission St. Not on Mission and 22nd St., where she said they fried the pigeons who lingered outside in front.

Sitting across from us at a too-long table, she licked her fingers between each bite and complained about the hospital food. She said it all tasted like bad nothing. I got hungry for the first time since the fire, watching her eat. I'd been too shaky to taste any of my food for the past two days since. Her eyes were larger than looked comfortable for her head and she talked over herself before finishing a sentence. They had called it *manic*. She complained about the cooking class she'd taken earlier in the day in the ward. *They only let us use plastic utensils. How the hell am I supposed to cut anything with this?!* She began to rub the cutting edge of the plastic knife she'd used to spread butter then grape jelly then strawberry jelly onto the soft inside of her cracked biscuit across her wrist, mockingly. When she pulled the knife lightly back and forth on her wrist, she flipped her tongue out the side of her mouth and played dead. There was still jelly on the knife and I was scared it would get on her white clothes. I covered Malik's eyes. He pinched my hand away and went back to being invisible. A nurse rushed over and didn't hesitate to pull my mother up into a tight hold like you do a child for their own good. I held my breath until my mother surrendered. The nurse pried the knife out of my mother's hand.

It wasn't long before my mother said she felt tired and that Malik and I should go home. She didn't acknowledge that she'd tried to burn our house down. I don't know if she'd heard I was inside that day, skipping sixth period. She stood up before us and pulled us into tight hugs while we were still in our seats. I could smell her hair. It still smelled like fire. I inhaled a full mouth when she bent her head to hug me and I disappeared into her white, rough canvas shirt.

Tanea Lunsford Lynx is a third generation born Black San Franciscan. She is a multi-genre writer currently working on a novel called Sanctuary City, which explores the effects of grief for the last 3% of Black San Franciscans left in the city.

For Shadow
an excerpt from Spiritower
Ilana Masad

Blocked and bleeding Steph is blind, deaf and dumb to the bell tolling in the chapel, to the bee dying on the windowsill, to the drip-drip-drop of coffee as it leaks out of the pewter mug that she had called up from one of her stories and made reality in an Oxfam on a hot summer day. She holds her hands over her mouth and bites them, pondering cannibalism.

—Nat do you think it's true we taste like chicken? I don't taste like Nat, wake up, wake up already Nat.

Out of a pool of drool and night sweats rises Nat. He is a shadow of a giant rather than the monster itself, the hilt rather than the blade, i.e. threatening, sort of.

—Nobody I know ever tasted like chicken, Nat says.

—But you haven't really ingested people, only parts of them, only temporarily, yes, yes, that's good, only temporarily ingest and then disgorge...

Fingers trembling, she reaches out for the keyboard as behind her the cramped room's walls grow closer together with Nat's stretching, filling out the empty space. Her womb yields and the fist pumps inside it. Liquid flows down between her legs into the small cup lodged tightly inside her, folded in on itself. There are people who drink blood, she recalls. She wonders if her liquid is bloody enough to tempt vampiric wannabes. Isn't there something holy about womb blood, woman blood, almost-potential-baby blood, something sacred, blessed, even if Eve and every woman after was a

—Sinner, we're all sinners, Steph whispers, her fingers typing blindly at the frozen, broken computer.

—You started early today, Nat doesn't ask.

Steph is deaf-blind-dumb though she speaks through her lips and sees through her eyes and hears through her ears but her senses add up to nothing since the most important thing is gone gone gone. Why not show Nat the pills, why not share, have a party, she is laughing now and happy because she has a Nat to share things with, and he is saying oh bugger pushing her off the bed and telling her to vom on the floor and not in bed if she has to while he gets her water from the loos.

Sleep is like flying when she does it. But there is nothing like her craft, and her craft is blocked, taken away in a dream of hunting-feuding men fighting over land and trees and deserts so desolate and dry and ugly that nobody wants to live there anyway. Except it is her home, that desert, they are walking all over her, over her birthright and lifeblood. Her womb-blood her fearblood her fear her frown, her furrowed brow, her thoughts and throat threatened, taken by these men these men, mean men, what do they mean these men? Lie on your back says a voice.

Not lying not lying I'M NOT LYING she yells. They're not lies a pack of lies I'm not a pack of liza dear liza... There's a hole in the bucket dear liza dear liza there's a hole in the bucket dear liza a hole. A whole. Not whole. Holy. Am I holy, holey, wholly myself Nat am I? Where did my words go where Nat?

Where were we when we wanted what we were?

What where who… white? White. Wh-wh-water. Water? I'm thirsty.

—I'm thirsty.

—Mornin', eh? What a bloody morning you gave me. Witch.

—What

—I said bitch!

—I'm thirsty Nat. Please?

He gets up and paces unevenly out of the three white curtains that surround and close her off. The curtains are held up by metal rungs and rings and a cracked grey ceiling above it all that reminds her of rainclouds and she wants the cracks to open like the rocks that Moses broke with his cane. Was it him who did that, that blessed stubborn man who never got to see the home he always wished for? Just like her, she knows she won't, she will never get a cabin in the woods with a dog and typewriter and all her needs taken care of by a god or at least the people who believe in her words enough to believe that the drips and drops and dabbles on the page (and what were the tablets if not the pages of the ancients) are sacred in some way or another.

Water comes in the form of a nurse made up of many percent of the stuff who also happens to be holding a cup filled with it who begins to check for vitals and fevers and liquids and Steph wants to point out that she too is made of water but that her thirst is still there, even though, even so. She drinks and keeps silent, allowing her arms to be checked for puncture holes which aren't there. Her skin is perfect, pure as seashells worn smooth by wave upon wave of salt water pounding on a seashore of gritty grainy sand dunes.

Ilana Masad is an Israeli-American fiction writer, book critic, and PhD candidate at the University of Nebraska-Lincoln. Her work has appeared in The New Yorker, McSweeney's, the Washington Post, the LA Times, NPR, Tin House, Printer's Row, Joyland, and more. She is also the founder of The Other Stories, a podcast that makes it just a little bit easier for writers to get heard.

Cuckoo Clock
an excerpt
Whitney Porter

But back to my mother, and how it seemed by remaining in my lesbian state, that it had caused her nothing but misery.

And at 22 when I announced I would be moving out after quitting college to work in a restaurant, this did nothing to alleviate her concern for my preference for pussy.

"You are working in a goddamn cafeteria. How can you tell me it doesn't matter that you're a lesbian!" she screamed.

Yet when I tried to explain, that a restaurant and a cafeteria were not the same thing and that even if they were, it had nothing to do with my being a lesbian it made no difference to her. To her my recent vocation and upcoming relocation had everything to do with her belief in my desire to spend my days in the various snatches of women in the greater Houston Metropolitan area.

My mother told me go to hell then slammed the car keys, then a bread plate, then a dirty set of silverware, then a pair of sunglasses calamitously down on our beleaguered and creaky kitchen table. And there I was paralyzed in our living room. Three over stuffed suitcases spilling over my feet, and a tote bag of toiletries clutched in my sweating palm. And right then I could see it, what was eating her up, what was killing her from the inside to the out—that in the dark recesses of her demented mind, that loopy wheel well turning in her brain, she thought that somehow this imaginary act of me eating out "EVERY SINGLE WOMEN IN TOWN" would somehow dietarily dilute my drive to succeed. Which meant it would keep me from becoming a real live grown person, with a college degree, a husband, a child and a house. All the things she thought would keep me safe. All the things she thought had kept her safe.

"I could never do that. Do what you are doing." My mother said looking downright eerie with her face shadowed through the mini-blinds, a glint of slotted sunshine splitting her face in two. "I had to get married. I had to have kids. I couldn't just sleep with women all day."

No doubt this is what she thought I'd do all day. How she imagined I would bide my time in my new apartment. That I'd get up in the morning brush my teeth, go back to bed and start my day of lesbian debauchery. Only taking time out from my perpetual muff diving to grab a sandwich for sustenance, then around 6PM, when I'd finally have to come up for air. Beat from a hard day of "making my mother's life a living hell," because according to her that's what I lived for, I would then retire my dental damn to the bathroom receptacle, and punch out for the day. Because what else do lesbians do other than depress their mother's and perform oral sex on each other like it's a job?

Oh this stubborn uncomprehending, angry despairingly stupid mother, with bunions the size of battleships, now limping her way to the foyer, in tears and I too was in tears, she slumped heaving on the stairwell, the rhinestones from her awful macramé sweater, dewy with her tears, and me now abandoning my suitcases with my face pressed against the dining room table, sobbing on the good mahogany. All the things she had done for me, half her teachers pay down the drain, all that tutoring, all that therapy, and for what. "You're still a damn dyke!" What should she have done different? What more could she have done. My mother asked me beseechingly. Her head plowed into her fist. And right about then, no kidding, the sound of the cuckoo clock chirped through our hyperventilated sobs, like the fucking omen it turned out to be. Oh the irony of ironies. That this shitty clock purchased for pennies at a flea market in East Houston, this cruddy vaguely wooded wonder, with a plastic bird with its plastic yap, this pathetic balding obnoxious bird, with tufts of glued on yellow and red feathers, how it encapsulated my pathetic life, with 10 perfectly placed cuckoos.

Whitney Porter is a 2016 Lambda Literary Fellow. Her work has been published an many now defunct webzines and literary magazines, such as Battered Suitcase, Metazen and Ping Pong Literary Magazine. This year her work was included in the Writers Studio at 30 anthology, published by Epiphany. She lives in Brooklyn and will continue to do so until she can no longer afford it.

White Angel
an excerpt
Santiago Jose Sanchez

The riff of a pop song drifts up to our apartment from the street below. Matthew leaves me in bed and sits on the window sill, resting his chin on the bend of his knee. From the window, he finds the source of the riff, a group of boys marching across the street in song. Their arms drape around each other's waists and necks in drunken camaraderie, the lazy fall of the snow dusting their shoulders, and it's amazing, he thinks, how they harmonize, how they begin to sing for no reason other than to sing, and isn't that something to see, isn't that why he came here? The stained glass door of the falafel shop snaps close behind the a cappella group, and though he's too far to hear the snap of the door, Matthew is sure it has snapped. The atmosphere of the room loosens and expands. He continues sitting there. On the bed alone, I am left looking at the back of his head. He has found an opportunity to separate himself from me and he has taken it. I struggle to feel close to him as the street quiets and he doesn't return to me, and I feel how the weight of my disappointment descends on me, like blankets so heavy they take two people to lift, four hands working together, as I wait for the moment that he will look at me again. I feel around me, the sheets not as warm as they were a moment before, how I had expected so much of this, as if with him the secrets of my life would be revealed to me, but now that he is here, I find that nothing has changed and that nothing will. He is still himself as I am myself. The snow is beating down now and the little flecks are sticking to the glass. They glimmer. His brow is raised when he turns to me, passive yet proud, like a boy asking permission for something he already has—he has me, held in his eyes, ready to give him anything. I feel the room contract again. If that is all that love is, attention, I feel it spread out over me. He takes my silence as his permission. He turns to the window again, fixing his eyes in front of him towards some distant direction. He searches the horizon for hints that New Haven is still there, beyond the grey sheet of the night, as he saw it today for the time, as if it were possible that he had fallen into another universe the moment I held the door to my room open for him. He catches the glowing edge of a tower, and further away, the blink of a red light. He doesn't invite me to sit with him, to look ahead together. That is not the love I have known from him. I feel how his fingers flatten on the cold glass and tug the pane up a few inches, how he rubs off the excess moisture on his thighs and tugs again, managing to lift the rusty window halfway up. *It's cold,* he says, rubbing his hands up and down the length of his arms, and this too, I feel with my own hands. At twenty-nine, Matthew is still undeniably handsome. He keeps a lean, masculine figure. Pubes scale his navel above the brown briefs with the pink bleach stain across the crotch. He steps out of them in front of the window, his face turning a light shade of pink around his nose as if he can smell his sudden nudity. The pink in the middle of his face dissipates into pallor as it radiates out to his forehead, where grows his mane of tossed-back, wavy hair that my mother had donned with an irresistible Americanness when she called him white angel. He blows his nose into his underwear. His arm draws a long, lazy arc as he tosses them to the ground. Once on the floor, the underwear begins to unfurl, the snot stretching out in a thin silver line, that snaps, leaving the sullied piece flattened and gooey in the shadow of his luggage. I try to understand how he has packed his life into this suitcase, how in a way it is his life that is leaning against the wall by the radiator. Tonight won't end with me driving back to my mother's house across Miami and flying back to Yale the next morning, as I had so many times over the last two years. He would be there in the morning and we would be here again the following night. The wind wraps around him, enters the room. The glossy pages of the magazines spread open across the floor. He is trying to show me how strong he is, how much pain he can take. I remember how in Miami he had stared at the sun. I pull the duvet up to my chin, determined to make a safe place below the fabric. The room expands. The cold cuts my lungs as I inhale it. My attention is sharp and expansive. I catalogue the details of this room. The radiator is clicking. The poorly hung paintings sway, scraping against the wall. I find that there is a moment of stillness after the wind leaves, when the pile of hangers on the floor spreads out under its own weight, stirred by some imperceptible change in the energy of the room, our room, and before the next wind hits. To my surprise Matthew sticks his arm outside. In an instant, the snow coats his fingers in little white gems, and through the window, it doesn't look like his own hand anymore, the same way his father didn't look like himself in the casket. You see death once and you see it everywhere, he thinks. It changes you. It's devastating. After the funeral, Matthew emptied his place in Miami and returned with all his belongings to the small town north of Tampa where he grew up. For the three months that followed, he lived with his mother, filling, however imperfectly, the void left by his father. He took a part-time at the Main Street diner, a small, stubborn place, where the same townies gathered every day at five, the same place where his mother had worked at as a young woman. He remembers the old jukebox unplugged in a corner, creaking, threatening to come back to life. He notices he's shaking. Goosebumps are rising out from his skin. The blue light of the parking garage across the street snags on those little puckers, turning them into patterns all along his shoulders and triceps. It's like he's made of marble with his mottled skin. Two more boys are crossing the street, silent this time. He wonders to himself, how much pain can one person take? Between the funeral and now, we talked almost every night on the phone, only as young lovers and the hopeless do. We would narrate the ephemera of our days to each other, like the customers that left him bible quotes instead of tips, and I would tell him about my classmates, on any given day when actually I did make it to class. When our days were fully dramatized, we would talk about our shared past that had accumulated during my visits to Miami over the last two years. We would talk about when we first met, how I had complained at the restaurant and gotten us a free bottle of wine, how I was definitely one of the top three fucks he had ever had, about how fun that first night had been, years ago, when we cut lines on top of his laptop and fucked until the light outside said it was morning. We bonded as only two desperately lonely people do. It was easy, real, like sinking into a familiar feeling. We determined that our sadness was like a weather pattern retreating and descending at a whim; that it was one long, sad wait, Life--and he was someone to wait with, to live with; it's snowing, really snowing and that is how the the snow feels, Matthew thinks at the window before he shuts it for the night. He crosses the room, leaving two imprints of his hands on the glass, where they will remain long after he is gone. He turns the light off. The shadow of Matthew tumbles into bed with me. He flattens out on his back, bending a pillow under his head and tucking his arm beneath. His armpit offers a wiry bush of golden hair dampened with the earthy, sour smell of him. After a moment, he turns to me and says, *I'm dead.* I lean into him in the dark, and it is like all the lights in the apartment are switched as his ripe smell lights my lungs, and I say, simply, *Me too.* I take hold of my white angel's hand, the one that had temporarily worn a glove of snow, and warm it against my lips. *What did Ms. Luz have to say about all of this?* he asks. I disband his hand from my lips, responding, *to be nice.* I leave out that I haven't told her that it's not just a visit, that we live together now. He raises his arm above us, stroking the top of my head. I feel him shift inwardly, and to fill the silence, to bring him back, I laugh, saying, *like she needs to remind how to behave.* He doesn't laugh as I expected him to. I'm reminded that sometimes these reflections about my mother and me make no impression on him, or if they do that he doesn't show any sign of it, leaving me embarrassed, feeling like I think about my mother too much. Like I try too hard. Like I'm vain. As if he can feel me beginning to spiral, Matthew, says, *lol, shut up,* and then, *here, let me hold you.* He turns me onto my side. His arm slides under my neck and folds over my collar. He drags me into his grip, the stubble of his chest meeting my soft skin with a sharp, yet pleasant pain. I press his hand, still cold, harder into my chest. I press harder, like the harder I press, the closer I will be to feeling what he feels. In his grip, I find his body to be larger than I remembered it, or perhaps, my body is smaller than I have known it. There is no greater joy, no higher purpose for love than survival. This is only the beginning to the rest of our lives, I think, stroking the line of his jaw, like it will always be there, behind me. *That's my ass,* he whispers, and I can't help but feel the crassness of his possession, or the ease with which I disown my body in responding, *I belong to you.* He pulls his arm out from under me, reinvigorated by the scope of his ownership. This young man is his. My head readjusts to the absence of Matthew and for a moment I can see myself on the other side of this night, of this relationship, alone in this bed again. He reaches between my ass, spreads the halves apart with his thumb and middle finger. The sudden exposure shoots a current through the center of me. It is like electricity. It is everything. I feel the sheets rising and falling, as he strokes his dick with his other hand, in a rhythm, time reduced to the intervals between the strokes. He drums my hole and the skin springs back to meet his finger. He gathers the saliva in his mouth and spits it on his palm. He lubes the opening. The supple sound of me yielding fills the room. He grabs my hip bone with both hands like an instrument and his cock directs itself between my thighs, in, then out, then in, then he sinks into me like a rod into a bucket of water. After our phone calls, he and his mother drank several bottles of red wine in their backyard. A fire crackled in an iron pit, the legs of which were uneven and the flames swayed in their direction; they liked it that way, the warmth, the jokes and laughter, of what they would look with their skin charred off, as victims of the fire. They talked of the trivial events of Central Florida, of the things that happened only on that stretch of the peninsula: the prom queen who joined the Mermaid Show, the iguanas falling catatonic from the trees, and the new retirement home—the largest in Florida. I imagine him on one of these nights telling her: *Ma, I'm leaving.*

Santiago Jose Sanchez is a writer and photographer based in Brooklyn, NY.

Debris of Twin
an excerpt
Lizzie Tran

"There is a war coming," the jeweler said to my mother as he polished the delicate golden necklace. In the dusty sunlight of the small room, the jeweler looked like a tiny dragon, fussing over his treasure. My mother nodded. "I know." The man's short, fleshy fingers were crusty and wrinkled from age and labor, and the seashell necklace looked otherworldly in his hands. "If you don't hide this necklace well, it will be taken from you," he continued as if my mother had not answered. He placed the necklace on the table, carefully next to the ocean seashell my mother had brought. She nodded, satisfied. The two looked identical.

**

I used to drag my name behind me, a shadow that weighed at least as much as I did. I tried not to look behind me; I moved forward the way prisoners stop thinking of their chains. The heaviness of movement becomes like breathing air, rhythmic, instinctual. People stopped asking me about my name once I changed it. I was in the second grade.

**

Living in a Vietnamese family turns you inside-out. People called me Isabelle on the outside of the home; my parents called me Tuyen on the inside. Before they called me Isabelle, they pronounced my name "Twin."

Years later, I heard "Two-yen." I was always asked to say my name in Vietnamese. This confused me; are you asking me to say *Isabelle* in Vietnamese? Because *Tuyen* is already in Vietnamese; are you asking what my name sounds like on the inside? And then I would say it the way it sounds to my ears, the way it bursts on my parents' tongues, the way it echoes from the mouths of an ancient Vietnamese tribe: it means boundary, a line between good and evil, right and wrong, war and peace. *Tuyen* is an inside name, is home, is the labyrinth of tongues and voices and ears and memories. I said it thousands of times, but on the outside, no one could hear it, no one could repeat it. It's a line, a boundary from the inside to the outside, People would smile, give up, and just say, "Sorry. I will just call you Twin."

**

Isabelle is a warm cloak, a thing that makes the outside feel comfortable, a dress code. It is easy for them to say; it makes the name feel familiar in their mouths and on their tongues. It makes their bodies relax, it creates the spell of belonging. If they can relax, then I can relax—at least, until we open our eyes and remember that we don't look anything alike, that I am adopted, that my real name is not Isabelle but Tuyen, that my life is littered with twos and twins.

**

I left Vietnam in darkness; I left a tiny seashell necklace there. On the dock, holding my older sister and me, my mother cried. "Tuyen! Where is the gold seashell necklace I hid in your shirt? I was going to use it to pay for our passage!"

In case we were stopped by thieves on the way to the boat, my mother had sewn the gold necklace into a hidden pocket of my shirt. In her desperation, she had demanded an answer from me when I was less than a year old and could give her none. Whether the necklace had slipped into land or sea, I couldn't tell her.

She used her wedding ring as payment instead, plus 5 ounces of twenty-four karat gold bars as a ticket for each person. She set my sister and me down near the water for a minute to pay, and in that minute, I fell into the sea. Was I looking for the necklace? Was I searching for a fish? My parents never looked at any ocean the same way after that.

And so I wasn't born afraid of the ocean. My father was a sea dragon; in the years before the War, my home was a paper boat where my mother used to come down the mountain to the shore and meet him. When the War ended and we were exiled, a boat made of wood—the boat my mother's wedding ring paid for—took us from the gentle waters of Biển Đông (East Sea) to a place of jagged rocks like broken teeth, and waves that could knock someone into darkness.

**

I have a twin still living in Vietnam. She has been married for ten years to the young man who owns the grove of coconut trees seventeen acres east of my parents' land. She never left Vietnam in 1979; at the last minute, my mother did not have enough gold with her to gain passage on the boat that night. She dreams of her twin's life in the United States, what her life might have been like if she had left on the boat that night. Would she have died? Would she have gone to medical school? Would she have married a woman? She secretly loves Long, the woman who owns the medicine store on the edge of town. Instead, she writes songs and poems for two of the most celebrated male poets-song writers in the country; she is the best cook of *canh chua* within a thirty mile radius, and she has four children— Tuyet, 9, Minh, 8, Tuyen, 6, and Xuan, 5.

**

I didn't understand love and loss in the second grade. I only knew that when it came time to choose my American name, I wanted Isobel's name, a girl in my class I could never speak to. I couldn't say her name out loud to her, but I wanted to hear my teacher say it, other people say it, and maybe even she could say her own name to me. And maybe I could finally find my voice. Instead, my parents spelled my American name *Isabelle*, and I tried to tell them it was spelled incorrectly, but they laughed and said, "No one will ever spell your name right if you spell it as *Isobel*. Isabelle is more common. Do you want to spend the rest of your life correcting the spelling of your name?" *Yes*, I did not say to them. *Yes, I am willing to spell my name to everyone, to hear everyone else spell it back to me, to say it back to me, as long as Isobel will say it, and I can hear myself speak, and I can hear her speak.*

**

There is another Tuyen in Vietnam, who did not come to the United States, and did not get married to the young man who owns the grove of coconut trees seventeen acres east of my parents' land. In 1979, she had slipped into the dark seawater the night my mother was looking for a golden seashell necklace as payment for our passage on the boat. Although my mother instantly jumped in after her, my mother was not a good swimmer. She nearly died trying to save her baby daughter, not quite one year old, and the man who collected gold as tickets felt sorry for her. He helped her out of the water, but they could not find the baby Tuyen. To this day, my mother is haunted by her lost daughter, swallowed by the sea.

**

My mother is a sorceress. Her words cast spells that change the hearts of men, the direction of the wind, the outcome of War. She has merged with her dead daughter, her heart extended into a space between sleeping and waking, a realm of magic. There, the voice of the sea Tuyen can be heard, the one still caught in battle, a whirlwind of soldiers and hand grenades and the screams of mothers. They reach, in vibrations, the walls and ears of a second-grade classroom where a girl has lost her name.

**

My mother is pregnant and walking through the jungle near Saigon, crying my father's name. I can taste the ash of smoke on my tongue as my mother wails, holding her belly as if her baby might fall, her feet in torn shoes. I feel the bite of twigs and leaves as she walks. I can smell the death of bodies piled on bodies. Another hand grenade flies past her, the heat sizzling against her left arm. It bursts through a tree, flinging men and women in all directions. It's too much. The heat of the jungle, vibrating with death, engulfs her. Darkness ohe vertakes her, and she falls, clutching her baby belly.

**

I wake suddenly from a dream about my mother. Sleep is still all over me,
invisible and sticky as spider webs, shadows in my eyes, whispers in my
mind. My body is cold and hot; sweat drips from my neck to the damp
pillow beneath my head. I swallow and my mouth tastes like salt. I inhale
and the air gives me no relief. War fills my body.

**

I dreamed of a medicine store at the edge of town, where my twin sister
first walked in as a child. She was eight years old, the same age as the
owner's daughter. The smell of dried herbs and wood furniture was in the
girl's hair when she leaned forward to examine the golden seashell necklace at my sister's throat. Sunlight split across her lap, and her feet felt
warm against my sister's leg. "I like your necklace," she said. "Do you want
it?" my sister asked. Laughter filled the room. The girls looked up at their
mothers, who were talking about which medicines to take for scar therapy.
"Yes," the girl answered, "But I won't take it from you. It looks like a real
shell from the ocean." "It *is* from the ocean." The girl smiled. "My name is
Long." My sister smiled back. "My name is Tuyen."

**

The medicine store never changed, even after the War was over. Unlike
many of the homes and stores that splintered and disintegrated from
fire, robbery, abandonment, new administration, the medicine store was
untouched by the ravages of War. Maybe that was the reason my twin
could enter the store and inhale its warm, dried-herb smell like she was

taking her first breath of air. Maybe that was the reason she smiled every time she saw Long behind the counter, folding medicine into pink paper packages and glass jars. Maybe that was the reason when Long reached across the glass counter to hand her teas and pho herbs and remedies for the ache in her left arm, she would feel cotton catch fire in her throat and her spine coming apart.

"I have a secret to tell you," Long whispered in my twin's ear.

My sister became dizzy with anticipation. She leaned in close, inhaling the sunlight from Long's short cropped hair. "I'm listening," she whispered back.

"Your parents bought poison from my mother after the War ended."

**

Long means dragon. I dreamed of her heart as I did any other woman's, as I did my mother's, trai tim, tim, the pitter-patter of love sounding through the rain. I dreamed within the mind of my sister as she ached, loving a woman who had poisoned the memory of her parents. From the moment Long told her about how her mother sold our parents poison, Long transformed into the dragon that occupied her name. My sister would never see this woman in the same way again: she would dream of her lithe body moving through the bright dust of sunlight in her tiny medicine shop, covered in gold coin-scales; she would dream of the smoke ribbons rising from her nostrils like someone breathing out poison, or a final breath.

**

I felt, not for the first time, that my twin dreamed of me, too. It was like sleep-walking through a mirror that faced a mirror, reflections infinitely unfolded into frightening vulnerability. I felt her in the moment I first touched Rona. It was only my hand against her hand, inadvertent touch, but I suddenly felt Rona's skin in the mind of my twin, the warmth of it, the movement of it through impossible barriers of land and ocean and time.

"Impossible," my mother had said to my father, after she had finally found him in the concentration camps deep in the mountains. She kept shaking her head. "Impossible. Before I walked out of the city, looking for you—"

My father grunted his disapproval. "That was crazy what you did. You walked out into a battlefield!" He grabbed my mother's left arm, glaring at the large scar left by the hand grenade.

My mother ignored him. "I was pregnant with one daughter. *One daughter.* The doctor and I clearly only heard one heartbeat before I entered the battlefield. And now we hear two heartbeats, two sounds disrupting each other's rhythm."

"Are you sure there are two of them?" my father asked.

Heartbeats sounded in time with the sound of gunfire, and it was hard to hear if there was one heartbeat, or two, or a thousand against the cries of people dying, of babies being born. "War is a mystifying thing.," I whispered to their images in my mind.

Rona's eyes widened in surprise, and she said my name like a question.

Elizabeth (Lizzie) Tran is a high school English teacher, a mother of two magical little boys, a Lambda Fiction Fellow, and a Kundiman Fiction Fellow—a space dedicated to the cultivation of Asian American Literature. She has written newspaper articles about social justice for the Vietnamese American community in Orange County, California. She is a lover of nature and words, a Vietnamese culture that doesn't recognize her, people of color, and feminism. Currently, she is agonizing over a series of linked Vietnamese stories that reimagines Vietnam, myth, and war, while next to the ocean she can't breathe without.

YOUNG ADULT

Let me tell you a story
Laura Carpenter

I was born cursed with a powerful, angry spirit lodged inside me. At my first cry, the midwife crumpled in death and my mother went into a sleep from which she did not wake for two moons.

Three fierce sorcerers snatched me up, covered themselves in every protection they could, and tried to break the curse. When they failed at that, they tried to kill me. When they failed at that, they headed toward the ocean to cast me out to sea and let the ocean monsters deal with me. But the winter blizzards that accompanied my birth, in a time that should have been green with summer, were too great to let them travel that far. Weak as they were from their attempts to fight the curse, they came here, to this canyon at the edge of a valley, as far from anything as they could go.

The birds tell me that people beyond the canyon still speak of the curse, tell stories about the spirit inside me and the destruction he caused in his last life, but the birds, those erratic things with freedom to fly away when the weather changes, refuse to repeat the story to me. They say the spirit grows stronger at the telling. They say they will not contribute to more pain.

Despite the birds' refusal, the spirit grows stronger, his fury an ever-present vat of lava, always threatening to erupt and destroy all I love.

Each spring, my guardians, the three sorcerers who brought me here, who are the only people I have ever known, try to break the curse. Each fall my guardians and I reinforce the barriers around the canyon and the protections that keep my guardians alive. Each summer we remember the beauty of life, and each winter we pay tribute to the dead.

In between the rituals, there are moments when I forget about the curse, when the sky comes out after the rain and a rainbow tells me anything is possible. I love the canyon, love the trees who have befriended me, the wolves that have taught me how to hunt, and the birds that share stories of distant lands, even if they fly away when I ask about the origins of the curse.

I love the blue of the glacier at the northeast end of the canyon and the way sunlight hits the canyon's narrow, other end in winter. Though the barrier is thick with trees and thorns at the canyon's southern point, the stream finds its way under, finds its way out, and I wonder if I might leave someday too.

Then I walk home past the markers of the dead. The midwife at my birth, several unfortunate souls my guardians encountered on their journey to the canyon, some people who ventured too close to the canyon and the spirit struck by lightning, and those from the earthquake several years ago when my bleeding started. I don't even remember why I got so mad. Whatever it was, it wasn't worth it. The spirit tore out of me in a rage not seen since I was a toddler, shaking the ground so violently the earth split open. Sixty-seven people died across Yorden. Some in landslides, some as far south as Unity, caught in a tidal wave. Some were children.

I made markers for each of them. I talk to the markers and their spirits. Most don't talk back. I bow my head to the markers. I promise them I will break this curse.

They don't trust me. I don't blame them.

Every day I grow more determined to break the curse and more doubtful that my guardians and I can. The determination and doubt strike me like waves against the shore, alternating hope with despair.

This is my life. The spirit had his. His destruction may have been so great that chickadees refuse to speak of it, but I will be afraid no longer.

This spring could be the time I go free. Will you help me? Yes, you, out there listening to me. Together we could do it. Together we have a chance. Imagine, walking along the tundra, picking lion berries, hills upon rolling hills ahead of you. Imagine, wading through a cold rushing river and getting to the other side, a side you've never been to before. Imagine, meeting someone new and becoming friends.

I will tell my story. Mine. Over and over. To the moose, to the birch, to the mossy stones who pretend not to listen. I will tell my tale and gain power at the telling, until I am hoarse, until my cracked lips bleed, until it is not the birds that fear stories but the angry churn inside me, until I am free, until I am me. Me fully.

Laura Carpenter has published non-fiction pieces in recognizable outlets and fiction and poetry in small, little whispers you probably haven't heard of. She hopes one day to switch that dynamic and to fill your bookshelves with her characters. She lives in Anchorage, Alaska, with her wife and daughter.

Portage
an excerpt
Joanna M. Eng

I get paired with awkward Savannah during our skills session on the third day of training. As we wait to launch, she's twirling both of her lifejacket straps in different directions while shifting from foot to foot in her dorky purple tourist sandals. What a piece of work.

It might have been nice to make friends who don't go to my school, but everyone here kind of ignores me so far. I don't care, actually I'm glad for it, because I don't want anyone looking at my face today. Especially today. Because I've decided to do it.

Grandma has the night off, and we're ordering pizza. When she inevitably tries to get me to talk about any boys I might be interested in, or asks if I want to go dress shopping so I can be ready for the summer block parties, I'll say it. This time, I'll say it. I can't keep covering.

Ever since Candace dumped me, I just can't anymore. Can't do a lot of things.

We glide the canoe out and Savannah's in front. I took the back position right away, not giving her much of a choice. I want to steer things my way today. And Savannah better keep her mouth shut. The past couple sessions she's always had some annoying piece of advice to add to Miguel's instructions.

I step into the back of the canoe and propel us away from the edge and into the estuary. The rocking subsides as I center myself on the seat.

"Okay, let's practice that new stroke I showed you." Miguel does the motion in the air again with his paddle. "Paddler in the front, keep your paddle completely out of the water for now."

The three other intern canoes wobble behind Miguel's. In front of me, Savannah practices the stroke in the air, several times in a row, even though she's not the one who has to do it.

I shake my head at her and try the maneuver in action myself, savoring the way the water feels like a muscle wrestling mine. Our canoe swerves to the right under the power of my paddling.

"Nice job, Jade," Miguel calls out. "Now try that again, but this time, Savannah, do a regular forward stroke on the opposite side."

Savannah poises her paddle above the water, and when I do the steering maneuver again, she does her thing too. This time, the canoe moves forward and right at the same time, with smooth force. I have to admit, it's better being paired with her than some of those clunky, uncoordinated guys.

We practice several more times and then Miguel announces it's time to flip the canoes. He did tell us about a hundred times to make sure to wear bathing suits today, and I have mine on under my basketball shorts and tank top. "You'll have to figure out how to right the canoe and get back in. It's all about staying calm and working with your partner."

To our left, Teddy tilts his body to one side without warning and the canoe goes over. His partner, Dom, shrieks and curses as he splashes into the water, and his Yankees hat flips off his head.

Savannah turns toward me, grinning like she's finally facing a challenge worthy of her skills.

She points her thumb to our right side. "Okay, on the count of three, just step on this side of the canoe and then jump out!" she says, really upbeat. "Ready?"

I nod, even though I'm dreading hitting the water.

"One . . ."

We stand up, wobbling.

"Two . . ."

We both start shifting our weight to the right and the canoe rolls, too easily.

"Three!"

I watch Savannah leap several feet out and I try to do the same.

It's cold, all at once. I thought the life vest would keep my head out of the water, but with the impact of the jump, some water goes up my nose and burns. I blow out of my nostrils, trying to take the edge off the unpleasant sizzle that's worming toward my brain.

I turn around in the water to find our canoe, which is now lying upside down and drifting away from us, along with my paddle. Savannah jets toward my paddle—she of course already has a strong grip on hers—grabs it, and then swims toward the canoe. She puts one hand on the pointed end of the bow (or is it stern?), looking pleased with herself. I focus in on her and doggy-paddle over.

As soon as I'm close she starts in: "Okay, so there's gonna be an intense air seal and it's not as easy as it seems to turn the canoe over. The best thing is to pick it up from one end first, and that way we'll be able to dump some of the water out at the same time."

"Savannah! Savannah!" Miguel's voice cuts across the chaos that is four capsized boats and eight flailing teenagers.

Savannah looks over.

"Savannah, if you've already done this a million times, why don't you let Jade take the lead?"

"Of course, great idea," she says, nodding as if that's what she was going to do anyway.

I'm still breathing hard from being tossed into the water, but I reach for the boat and place my hand near Savannah's.

I look around and see that we're all still hanging on to the overturned canoes. Someone—probably Dom—says in a dramatic voice, "I'll never let go. I promise." Everyone starts cracking up at the line from *Titanic* and others cry out, "Rose!" "I love you, Jack." "I can't feel my body."

Savannah rolls her eyes, and says matter-of-factly to me, "Ready?"

I nod. I brace myself—which is hard when I'm in the water with nothing to stand on—and muster my arm strength to lift one end of the canoe against the strong suction. I let out a grunt as I tilt it just enough to get it off the surface of the water.

"Excellent," says Savannah, then goes to the other end to help roll it all the way upright.

Our canoe is still almost half full of water, but I look over at Teddy's and it's full almost to the top. He's trying to paddle with his hands while sitting in the bottom of the canoe, chest deep in water.

Savannah holds onto our canoe and tells me to climb in from the other side. I wrestle my way into the boat, rocking it a ridiculous amount as I land inside. Then I watch Savannah hoist herself in gracefully, almost in one motion.

She smiles at me, her hair dripping, and I notice a few freckles scattered across her nose just under the drops of drying water.

"Paddle high-five," she says, holding out her paddle toward me.

***

As Grandma takes her post-work shower and puts on one of her matching velour track suits—she has one in practically every color—I pace from the eat-in kitchen to the entry hall and back again, waiting for our pizza and chanting in whispers to myself. I'm fiddling with the knots on the drawstring of my mesh shorts the same way Grandma thumbs her rosary.

I've been practicing what to say for the past three weeks post-Candace. Actually, I had a whole different set of rehearsed lines during Candace, and another set pre-Candace. And I've had so many chances to tell Grandma, but I always let the moment slip into silence instead, or let her carry the conversation away someplace else.

You got this, I say to myself, picturing the encouraging smile Miguel gave us as we all tried to get our canoes upright while treading water this morning. *Even if I totally capsize tonight, I can make things right again,* I think, then roll my eyes. Candace would call out my complete cheese-ball-ness right now. But then again, Candace apparently didn't get me. At all.

The doorbell plunks and I swing aside the little cover on the peephole to see the same delivery guy who's been coming every week with our sausage pie for at least a couple years now, but still looks like he's about thirteen. I wrench open the metal door. I feel like I should know delivery kid's name by now, and maybe even invite him in for a slice. Instead I give him an extra smile and an extra dollar tip.

He beams back before I shut the door, and I feel energized to face Grandma, who's coming out of her room as I rest the pizza box on the stove, right on schedule.

She flip-flops her way over in her teal sweat suit, and places her hand flat on my shoulder, then measures it up to her own forehead. "You're getting so tall." She says this every couple weeks or so, even though I've been the same height since sophomore year. Maybe she's starting to shrink.

We sit down at the tiny two-person table with our first slice, me sprinkling extra basil and pepper on mine, Grandma propping hers up at an angle to drain the grease off.

"How was work?" I ask, my heart already pounding too fast.

Grandma launches into a story about a patient who had so many family members in the hospital room that it was hard to get close enough to the bed to take care of her. "And then they all ordered Indian food so the whole place smelled like curry. You could smell it down the hall. And you know I like to try all kinds of ethnic food, but certain smells just don't sit right in a hospital. You know what I mean?"

I resist rolling my eyes, and instead take some big bites, finishing half my slice, while Grandma takes a few small ones.

"So, Jadie, how was your kayaking internship today? Do you have any customers yet?" She's always calling it kayaking, but I'll let it slide this time.

"No, we're still in training. The public programs start next weekend."

"Right, right, I keep forgetting. So, how are the other interns? Have you met any nice boys?"

My alarmed pulse is up to my throat now. I thought I would at least get to finish one slice before getting into the talk about boys. "Oh, they're cool. There's a lot of interns, including this one random girl from Massachusetts."

"Where are the other kids from?"

"Oh, from around the Bronx or Manhattan. One guy's from Yonkers."

"Right, right. Who's this boy from Yonkers? Is he cute?"

I shrug, and finish my crust. I push my chair out and get up for a second slice. Before sitting back down, I take as deep of a breath as I can manage.

"So. I wanted to tell you something."

"Oh? Okay." She puts down her half slice and dabs at the edges of her mouth with her napkin.

"So." I try for a slight smile but my cheek muscles are not cooperating. "You know Candace?"

"Yes, Jadie, of course. She hasn't been over here in a while."

"Yeah, she probably won't be coming over anymore."

"Why? Is she alright? Did something happen to her?" She throws her napkin down on the table like she's about to jump into action. Grandma always liked Candace, probably wished I was more like her.

"She's fine. But—" I focus on the blobs of sausage on my pizza. "We don't see each other anymore. She broke up with me." I keep looking down at my plate.

"What are you saying, Jadie? She doesn't want to be friends anymore?" Grandma's voice is getting higher.

"No, Grandma. Candace was my girlfriend. We were dating." I make myself look up at her face and her mouth is wavering, not sure if it wants to be open or closed. "I wanted to tell you before but I . . ." I can't finish my sentence.

I go back to staring at my uneaten slice. Out of the corner of my eye I watch Grandma pick up her napkin again and fold it, and fold it, and fold it, until it's a tiny square springboard that she tucks under the edge of her plate.

Joanna M. Eng is a writer and editor who loves creating stories for all ages featuring characters who don't fit into neat categories. She lives with her wife and child in the New York City area, where she is constantly seeking out slivers of nature.

Project Novo
an excerpt
Soon Jones

There were only a few weeks left until Sojourner IV took fifty lucky passengers from the planet Novo back to their ancestral home of Earth, and Cassiopeia Yi was going to be one of those fifty even if it cost her her soul. But while other Novans were spending their life savings on lottery tickets for a chance at a seat, Cass was going to get there with blood.

She parked her truck by the edge of a hole boring down into the sand and clay. All morning she and her latest hunting partner, Dan Toh, had tracked a group of people with heavy artificial body modifications across the wastes. Except they weren't people anymore, Cass reminded herself. In the eyes of the law, they had lost their status as human beings when their bodies had become over sixty percent artificial. They were harvests now. Their remaining organs would be used to save the lives of those who could still reproduce and postpone the extinction date of Novo's human population. And every harvest she retrieved brought her another point closer to a ticket to Earth.

Cass slipped on her helmet and inserted a new oxygen canister in its back. She looked to make sure Toh had his helmet secure before opening the door of the truck and stepping outside into the oxygen-thin atmosphere.

"You waited for me. Everyone warned me you wouldn't," Toh said, sounding surprised.

"I won't do it again," Cass promised.

It was their first mission together and would probably be their last; her partners always left, disturbed by her willingness to leave behind her teammate at the first opportunity if she thought it would benefit her or end the mission quicker. She didn't see a reason to develop any comradery with her teammates outside of missions, either; she had gotten this far without friends, so why try now? She was going to leave them all behind anyway.

From the back of the truck, she and Toh took out harnesses and weights to block the tires so the truck wouldn't budge. From the reinforced front, they unwound two separate cables threaded with phosphorous string from the wench and dropped them down into the hole. She appreciated that Toh didn't try to talk to her like other partners had; he worked quietly and without needing direction. This was going to be an easy mission.

They helped each other into the harnesses and rappelled down the chasm. When the top of the hole was just a pinprick of light, her feet finally touched ground.

A tunnel opened before them, supported by beams of pieces of cut metal that were wedged tightly together, likely salvaged from ancient seed ships that had first brought humans to Novo. The floor had long been beaten smooth by the feet of countless people passing through. Cass followed the ghosts of their footsteps, turning on the night vision and camera functions of her helmet.

They entered a room large enough to hold a hundred people, with two exit tunnels burrowed into the hard-packed dirt walls. A few lights were half buried in the walls and ceiling, all turned off. Water bottles, bent screwdrivers, broken microchips, and random detritus were scattered all over the floor.

She went to the tunnel on her left, sticking her head inside and boosting the audio levels of her helmet, holding her breath to listen. She heard a distant echo of a sound like a foot scuffing or a cough. Without looking back to see if her partner was following, she ran in.

It took ten minutes before she spotted the three harvests, hands against the wall, moving as quickly as they could through the darkness without a light. They carried nothing and wore old, dirtied clothes. A young woman in the back was helping the elderly couple ahead of her move faster, pushing them from behind. A quick scan with the helmet interface confirmed their nonhuman status: 65%, 62%, and 73% artificial parts respectively, and many of those parts were in desperate need of repairs. There wasn't a lot that could be harvested from their bodies, but there were at least a few healthy major organs between them. If she caught all three of them, she would get enough points to be in the top ten of state-sanctioned hunters before the rankings closed and the winners were awarded with seats on Sojourner IV. Cass sprinted forward, pulling her tranquilizer gun out of her hip holster and raising it with both hands.

"Stop! Under the authority of the Senate, I order you to—"

The woman in the back twisted around and swung at her. Cass ducked out of the way and fired a tranq but missed, the bolt bouncing off the wall.

"Run!" the woman yelled, and the other two paused for a moment before taking off, tripping over themselves to get away.

Cass blocked the next punch and struck the woman hard in the gut. She crumpled and hugged her arms around her stomach, sucking in air like she was drowning, eyes wide.

"No! I'm pregnant!" she cried.

Cass paused. Then the woman flashed a wicked grin and punched a switch hidden in the dirt. A controlled blast collapsed part of the tunnel, blocking Cass off from the other two modders. She flared her nostrils, annoyed she didn't have any explosives of her own to blow the rubble away. She did quick calculations in her head: if she took another mission tomorrow, she could still secure a spot on the top scoreboard before the weekend.

The woman attacked her from the ground, tackling her around the waist. Cass kneed her hard and she screamed, falling to the ground again and trying to scramble away, but Cass was on her in a second and twisted the woman's arms around her back, cuffing her wrists.

"That was a good trick. I've never lost a modder before on a mission, and now I've lost two. Are you even really pregnant?" Cass asked.

"I am. You can test me!" the woman said.

"I don't have any pregnancy tests, but you'll have an opportunity to plead your case to carry to term to the harvesters when we get back to the city," Cass said, shoving the woman in front of her.

The woman laughed bitterly.

"You think they'll take care of my child after they carve me up for parts? There's plenty of babies who need organic transplants, too," she said.

Cass clenched her jaw. Why was she talking to this woman? All it ever did was complicate the mission. She didn't want to think about babies and transplants.

"They're not going to harvest a baby. Birth rates are too low," Cass said finally.

The woman just shook her head. Her breathing was ragged as she gulped in mouthfuls of air. Cass hesitated before taking a deep breath and pulling off her helmet and securing it over the woman's head, making sure the air canister was secure. She waited a few moments for the woman to catch her breath before pushing her back down the tunnel. After only a few steps her lungs started protesting, but she could abide the burn for now.

The only thing worse than having too many artificial parts was being infertile, and Cass had never gone through menarche. She had managed to bypass the mandatory fertility test in high school by breaking in after hours and manipulating her student records to buy herself time, but it wouldn't be enough. Dropping out and joining the hunters had only given her another five years or so before auditors would show up at her door to tell her it was time to pick a sperm donor and do her part in saving Novo.

She had to get a ticket to Earth, no matter what it took. Then she'd finally be free to live out her whole life without fear of ending up on a table, sliced up for whatever parts were viable to extend the lives of other, more fertile citizens. She told herself she would find a way to live with the guilt after she was safe on Earth, and most days she could almost believe herself. This was not turning out to be one of those days.

Toh finally caught up to them, eyes wide and angry.

"Where have you been?" Cass demanded.

"I should be asking you that! I was inspecting the entrance of the other tunnel and you left without telling me," he snapped.

"I told you I wouldn't wait," Cass said, then she gasped for air despite herself.

He looked from her to her prisoner, pointing at the helmet.

"What's this?" he asked.

"She's pregnant. If it's a viable fetus, we need to save it," Cass said.

"The other two?" he asked.

Why wouldn't he shut up? Where had the quiet Toh from earlier gone?

"She blew part of the tunnel. They escaped," Cass said calmly, trying to preserve breath.

Toh asked more questions, but she stopped listening and kept pushing forward. She tried to take as many even breaths as possible, but she was already feeling light-headed. She reminded herself that once they got back to the truck she could breathe in as deep as she wanted, as long as she wanted.

"Do you really think they'll save my baby?" the woman asked quietly, breaking through Cass's thoughts.

"Babies can't be harvested. Most likely it'll be raised in a pure organic's house. It'll be safe," Toh said gently.

Cass didn't know if any of that was true. She hoped so, for the woman's sake.

"My name is Abigail. Do you know what 'Abigail' means?" the woman asked.

"No, I don't," Cass said. How much further was the damn exit?

Abigail waited a beat before saying, "Neither do I. I'm going to die without ever knowing."

They finally reached their exit tunnel, the glowing cables still waiting for them. Abigail twisted around to face Cass, her eyes tearing behind the glass.

"Will you find out and tell my baby? Please, I'm begging you. I want my child to at least know my name," she said.

"If she won't, I will," Toh promised.

Abigail didn't look away from Cass.

"I want to hear you say it."

Cass clenched her jaw, pulsed the muscles, ground her molars into each other. If she was lucky, she'd be off Novo and flying to Earth before Abigail even started to show. Was it more merciful to tell the truth or to lie?

Cass picked the second option.

"I promise I will find out. I will tell your child when they're grown enough to understand," she said, and told herself that she could live with even this.

Then she shot Abigail in the upper thigh with a tranq so she wouldn't have to look the woman in the eyes anymore. She sagged in Cass's arms. Cass laid her gently on the ground, slipped the harness over Abigail, careful not to put pressure on the stomach.

"You go up with her first," Cass said to Toh.

"But you don't have a helmet," he pointed out.

She threw the harness at him.

"So hurry up."

He muttered under his breath while he put on the harness and attached to the cable, sending a command up to the truck to start pulling them up. Cass stayed at the bottom of the hole while Toh and Abigail were lifted to the surface, clenching and unclenching her jaw until it hurt as she watched Abigail become swallowed by the light.

She couldn't live with this.

Soon Jones is a pizza delivery driver by day and a writer by night. She is also an assistant editor at Moon City Review.

Cecil in Training
an excerpt
Charlie Miller

I wasn't always a boy.

Or, well, maybe I was.

Some people say they always knew. I didn't always know. Mostly when I was a kid I didn't really notice I had a body. I just kind of floated around, doing what I wanted to do. My parents never made a big deal out of me being a girl or anything. It was just, like, I had a vagina, so that's what I was, but they didn't force me to do anything I didn't want to do. Maybe they would have, if I hadn't been actually pretty into dolls and clothes and the color pink.

I dressed up barbies. I strutted around the house in my mom's clothes. I wanted my bedroom walls pink. I read a lot, and insisted on being Captain and bossing everyone around when we played pirates, and spent a lot of time narrating everything I did under my breath and performing weird monologues on the toilet. I was just a kid.

It's just that when everyone else started growing into their bodies, I didn't.

I mean, I did. I got boobs, and I got my period. But I never stopped feeling disconnected from it. I never stopped feeling like I was just floating around. Frankie and Lily Rose and the girls I knew at school started learning what they were "supposed to" do with their bodies — put on makeup, wear bras, kiss boys, find every flaw they could — and I didn't. It wasn't like they liked "girl" stuff and I didn't like "girl" stuff and therefore I wasn't a girl. The equation's not that easy. Lots of girls don't wear makeup or kiss boys or even wear bras. Lots of girls cut their hair short and wear boys' clothes.

It was just that while they found their bodies magnified, thrust under a microscope by every magazine and creepy old man in a ten mile radius, I was just...a ghost.

I started acting at school and at camp, because all I was anyway was a blank slate. I loved being villains, Ms. Hannigan and Rizzo and Ms. Baltimore Crabs, because I could inject them with big, full personality and anger and ridiculous costumes, all the things I didn't have — felt like I wasn't allowed to have — in real life. And also because deep down I thought maybe...maybe I really was bad to the bone, that simmering underneath my wispy school appearance was something absolutely terrible. Something selfish.

But when I wanted to be the dentist in *Little Shop of Horrors* in the spring of my sophomore year, I couldn't.

That role went to Michael Moretti, and I wasn't anything, because there was one female role, besides the Doo-Wop girls, and none of those roles were right at all. I was in the background.

When everyone looked at Michael Moretti and saw a dentist with a motorcycle and a big voice, they looked at me and saw...nothing.

That was when I fell into the pit.

Not literally. I didn't fall into the theater pit or anything, though that story would be a lot more fun to tell. The pit is a place where my brain can go.

It's like this:

I'm really bad at math. But my parents rode me hard about grades, made me terrified to ever do anything less than the best, so somehow I got through it, achieving impossible B's and even A's. But it wasn't easy. I know — stupid kid, wanting everything to be easy. In the old days we swallowed our pain until we choked to death. But what I mean is, it was harrowing. It kept me up crying at nights. I gave myself monster headaches. I was walking along a tightrope, and at every single step there was the possibility I'd slip. I'd fall into the darkness below. I wouldn't be able to crawl out.

That was how I was "being a girl." And after *Little Shop*, I slipped. Being in the pit is exactly what it sounds like. It's nothing, but it's everything, too. It surrounds you. You can't get up in the morning. You don't feel like crying. There are elephants on your shoulders and your chest and in your stomach, too, and still, somehow, you're empty.

You're nothing. You're a ghost.

It's not sadness. Sadness has reasons. Sadness has an expiration date. You can talk away sadness, or eat it away with ice cream and waffle fries, or watch it away with musicals. But the pit gobbles up everything you try to give it. It chews up your cheer-ups until there's nothing left of them, and it only gets bigger. You need something less everyday than french fries to fight it. You need bulldozers, or war horses, or wrecking balls.

Or, in my case, twenty milligrams of Lexapro and a new hormone.

Okay, it wasn't that simple. I also needed hugs from Frankie and Lily Rose. I needed my brother to say, "I always wanted a brother." I needed the doctor to say, "Alright, young man," and the camp director, Sam, to say, "Of course, dude, I'll follow your lead" when I told him how things would be different when I showed up this summer.

People want to hear something more than all that, or maybe something less. Cecil + trucks + football = boy is a lot easier to solve than Cecil + boy = Cecil — anger. Cecil + boy = Cecil — despair. Cecil + boy = Cecil + freedom + happiness + the whole world unfolding into something I have a right to join.

Things aren't perfect. My mom signed the papers for hormones, but my dad still calls me "Lila." My voice has mostly dropped, but I'll probably still have my boobs for a while.

But this summer, I'm out of the pit. Mostly.

I'm me, anyway.

Charlie Miller is a queer trans writer and student of Children's Literature and Library Science at Simmons College in Boston, MA.

A Fairy Tale
an excerpt
Miranda Schmidt

She still hears the wings at night. In that space between waking and dreaming where, for a moment, she has no shape at all, she can feel them: their hollow-boned strength, the rhythms of flight, the rustle of feathers in air.

Most nights they wake her and she startles back into her human limbs, solid and earthbound, a sleepless sixteen-year-old girls in a house of lost children all wearing the same brand of discount PJs. But some nights, fewer and fewer now, the sound bears her away into dreams. And that's when she flies.

You can't imagine it, what flying is. Not really. Not unless you've done it. Not unless you've felt the wind through your feathers, the power of wings to steer you through currents, the heady heights that linger just above the world.

The kids in Morgan's house, they look normal, but they aren't. They're lost and found things with half-memories of parents and homes and cradles and toys, once upon a time, before the other memories begin, the ones of water or air or woods, those memories that feel like dreams shot through with the deepest, most aching of longings.

By those who understand it, they're called stolen children. They're a part of a curse so old that only myth remembers how it began in the first place. They were taken once, but in this house at the edge of the forest, they seem returned. They seem happy and adjusted and so close to normal they almost believe it themselves. They go to school with everyone else. They play on sports teams and join clubs and put in college applications. And its only sometimes that they stay underwater for a moment too long, like Hazel did, wondering if holding her breath might bring back her lost gills. Only sometimes do they find themselves out on the lawn howl-crying like Tif, feeling the night on their faces and knowing that they are only half-here, half-real, half-children. It is only on some nights that Morgan dreams her wings and wakes perched on the attic windowsill ready to fly.

This is one of those nights.

She wakes to moonlight, to the chill autumn air on her face and, for a second, she thinks she's turned back. She feels her beak and talons. She feels her light wings and her old corvid mind urging her on to escape. Then she raises her wings to find only arms. She remembers her girl feet, her human skin, her weak mammal eyes. Her person brain kicks in to remind her of gravity. She steps off the windowsill and back into her bedroom, shivering in the cold October wind.

On these nights, she used to creep down to Hazel's room. She'd slip into her bed and they'd whisper about the times before they were human, about how gliding through water and gliding through air are the same, both relying on currents and instinct and knowing. Or when Hazel woke up feeling breathless, as if she were drowning in air, she'd slip up to the attic. Sometimes, the two girls would talk all night long. Sometimes they'd kiss until they fell asleep with Hazel's head on Morgan's shoulder and Moragan's arm wrapped around Hazel's body.

Tonight, Morgan doesn't know what to do now that Hazel is gone. So she does what she has all this last month since Hazel went missing. She goes downstairs and pulls on her boots and makes her way to the water. We watch her follow the river, searching. We watch her walk down to the estuary. We watch her stand alone on the shore and look out towards the ocean.

She waits, but Hazel never comes. Sometimes she thinks she never will.

But we know better.

Miranda Schmidt's work has appeared in Electric Literature, Triquarterly, The Collagist, and other journals. She lives with her wife and two cats in Portland, OR and is currentlyworking on a project inspired by shapeshifting fairy tales. You can read more of her work at mirandaschmidt.com.

What Happens Now
an excerpt
Nita Tyndall

I don't listen to the Evita cast recording (Patti LuPone, not Madonna,) on the way home like I have for the past month. Instead, I blast what I always do when I'm angry—old-school country. Rock helps, yeah, but there's nothing like singing along to Loretta Lynn when you're pissed off. No one does hurt like scorned country women. When Patsy sings, you can almost hear her crying.

Which reminds me, I have band practice tonight. Some of the guys from the Baptist church my dad goes to roped me into joining their country cover band on weekends, singing at this sad karaoke dive bar off Highway 64. It's fine, I guess. I get to put on the old-fashioned dress and the heels and the lipstick and pretend to be Patsy Cline for a night.

So okay, maybe it's better than fine. It's actually fun once I get past the drunk guys staring at my boobs while I sing.

But I have family dinner first. Not to mention a buttload of home-work and the fact that I promised Sarah I'd Skype her tonight.

God, I hope she answers. She's been cut short the last two times we've tried to Skype, once with a rehearsal she couldn't get out of, and once because her roommate invited her out. Never mind that we'd been doing bimonthly Skype sessions since she started college.

She's leaving you behind, I think, and then I try to forget that because all it's going to do is make me sad.

Dad's car is in the driveway when I pull in, Tammy Wynette on full blast. He's started this thing where he comes home early from work on Fridays so we can all have this family dinner, since it gets Mom out of her room and eating with us and he can actually feel like he's doing something.

I should cut him some slack. He is trying. She is, too. Meds and two years of therapy have helped her depression, but we all know there are good days and bad.

Too bad for Mom if her bad day falls on a Friday, though. Dad still wants us all to sit together at the dining room table we normally only use on Christmas, mental illness and homework be damned.

We eat promptly at six. It's Dad's compromise for the two sides of the family—his Italian side which won't eat until like, 9 p.m., and Mom's good 'ol Southern Baptist family who eat supper at 4:00.

Dad's cooking when I enter the house. No take-out on Friday nights, either. It's always a home-cooked meal Dad's got from one of Nonna Felicia's old recipe books. Dessert is Mom's side, cobbler or pie or a "dump cake" in the Crock Pot.

It's usually dump cakes. They're called that for a reason, and since you just dump all the ingredients in the Crock Pot it takes very little energy and still tastes amazing.

"Cast list go up?" Dad asks the second I step in the kitchen. He's got lasagna sauce simmering on the stove, noodles boiling away.

"Yup," I say, setting my backpack by the table and grabbing a wooden spoon so I can sneak a taste of the sauce. This is tradition, too, me trying to taste everything before it's ready.

"And? Are we gonna get to see you stand on that balcony?"

I don't respond. Bite my lip, set the tasting spoon down. Dad notices and turns to me.

"Hey. You okay?"

"Not playing Evita," I mutter, and the frustration at the unfairness of it and Phoebus's comments just comes back and suddenly I'm actually crying.

Dad stands there, holding a spoon. He's not great with emotion. I grab a paper towel and blow my nose into it, comically loud.

"Are you still in the show?" he asks after a minute, and I nod.

"I'm the Mistress."

"That's not so bad," he says. I glare.

"I only get one song and then I'm just ensemble for the rest of time," I say, and I cringe at how childish I sound.

"Did Phoebus give a reason why?" Dad asks, and seeing that I'm not still crying, turns back to the stove.

I look down at my shoes. Mom enters the kitchen at that moment. "What's all this?" she says, looking at Dad cooking and my still-red face.

"I didn't get the part," I mutter, and she immediately sweeps me up into a hug.

"Oh sweetie," she murmurs, and strokes my hair like I'm five, and I feel selfish but my first thought is that she smells like she's showered today which means today is an okay day which means in this moment I can allow myself to be sad and allow her to take care of me.

"It sucks," I sniff, and pull back. "And he kinda said it was because of my weight, which…"

My mom puts her hands on my shoulders and looks at me. "He said that?"

"Well, no," I admit. "He said I didn't look the part, but that's… I know what he meant."

Fuck. I shouldn't have said anything. They're staring at me and I shouldn't have mentioned that right when we're all about to eat dinner, because weight is a sore spot in this family, particularly whenever Nonna Felicia comes over.

Dad brushes his hands on his apron. "The girl playing Evita, is she good?"

"Jack…" Mom starts.

"It's just a question."

"Yeah," I say. "She is. She's really good."

"Well there you go, then," Dad says, and my face just burns even hotter. He grabs a pan out of the cabinets and begins laying lasagna noodles in it like the matter is settled, and my mom looks at me pityingly and I mumble something about homework before running upstairs to avoid both of them.

Nita is a tiny Southern queer from North Carolina. She writes YA, works with tech, and lives with her girlfriend and their pets.

Dark
an excerpt
Daryn Wilde

"Well, look at that!" is the first thing my father says. "*My* efficacy just went up 100%!"

Asshole.

My lips apparently aren't listening to reason yet, because they mutter the word just as vehemently as I thought it.

My father laughs.

"Well, yes, darling. That's kind of our thing." He peers into my eyes. My eyes that are a mirror to his now. My eyes that were so much like my mother's eyes, every moment of my life before. But… Before I knew I wasn't a 1950s housewife. Before I knew I wanted Xena the Warrior Princess to rescue me, instead of boring, old Prince Eric. Before Avery. Before… Avery.

I can't see her face behind her hair, her head bowed, her body tied to a chair and, *God,* what they've done to that beautiful body, bruised that beautiful skin, broken that skin to bloody and weeping, even though she is silent… I'm glad my eyes are black as a pit, black as night, black as rage right now. Sea foam green wouldn't be tough enough to handle this shit. Sea foam green would cry. Black glares at my father and can see him as something more than that, something separate.

He is my father, yes. But he is also an asshole. All those times before when he was an asshole, that wasn't just a businessman being a businessman. Some businessmen manage to be decent human beings beneath their $3,000 suits. Some manage to be even good men, maybe. It's just *this* one that was always an asshole. I was just too young to see it before.

This is a moment, I guess, of growing up.

The moment you look at your father, and you see a man, and you can judge him as such.

This one, this one is a bad man.

Whatever else he is, he's a bad man.

My father is nodding like he can hear my thoughts, but I think it's just my squinted eyes and snarling lips that speak to him. And he, the bastard, is still smiling.

"I think you're going to fit right in," he tells me.

"I don't want to fit in," I growl. "I want Avery back. And I want you to go to hell."

He laughs again.

"Oh, darling. There is no Hell. The Christian myths are a pretty murky interpretation of things. They heard 'Dark' and 'Light' and made a wild assumption to 'Evil' and 'Good' from there. Frankly, it was downright irresponsible interpretation. You have a duty, as an interpreter, to portray the essence of the message accurately, without undue influence from your own culture's mores. Those Christians who first scribed the story..." He tuts.

"Interpreters?" *What?*

"It'd be like a story of a three-legged cat, but you've only ever seen cats with *four* legs, so you just go ahead and transcribe the story as being about a cat with four legs. Maybe it was important that the cat had only *three* legs. Maybe it makes it an entirely different tale!"

My mouth is hanging open. I can feel it. I just can't do anything about it.

My lips are expressing my utter bewilderment.

Even if myself would rather keep it to myself.

My father laughs again.

He seems much happier as a Dark man than a man-man. The man I grew up with almost never laughed.

" 'Dark' and 'Light' aren't the same as 'Evil' and 'Good'," he summarizes. "And where we come from is neither Heaven, nor Hell." He smiles at me *almost* like a father should. "I imagine you'll get to see for yourself someday." The change is quicksilver as his smile slides into a smirk. "Not today though!" he concludes. "Please," he gestures to a stool next to Avery, "have a seat."

"I'd rather not."

There's blood splattered on the floor around that stool. Not *on* that stool because somebody was *sitting* on it while the blood splattered, watching, watching as Avery was hit so hard her blood went flying... I don't think I want to sit in the middle of a cement ocean of her blood. And I don't think I want to sit on a stool where my father sat while she was bleeding, where he gave the orders to *make* her bleed.

But, "I'd rather you did," my father counters. And he gestures to the stool this time with the gun instead of his hand.

"You can't shoot me," I tell him. I remind myself. "You need me."

My father nods along again. "Yes," he agrees. "We'd really like you to teach us some of your very particular skills." He purses his lips. Pretends to consider. "But we don't really need you *whole* for that, do we?"

"I – " No, I suppose they don't.

"So I can shoot you in the leg," my father continues like I hadn't interrupted. "Hell, I can shoot out both kneecaps so you *have* to sit. Or you can just sit."

It seems like a concession to sit. It seems like bowing to a false idol of fear.

It'll hurt like hell, but Light can –

I start to wonder if my father really can read my mind when he says, "At some point, even Light can't heal you, Catherine. At some point an injury stops being something broken and becomes just a part of your body. Something that *is*. You can't heal a body from its natural state. So even Light can't heal an injury that has grown so old it is merely a natural nuance of the body." He smiles, almost gently, if his eyes were capable of that. "So, I'll ask you again, Catherine: Please, sit. Or would you rather never stand again?"

My father would cripple me for wanting to stand, when he wants me to sit.

Wilde

Such a small difference. Such a petty difference.

And –

He's planning to take me with him.

If he and Greg are 'risking the run to Italy', like I heard them say earlier, then I'm on the plane too.

Light would have no opportunity to heal me.

Not for months.

And.

God.

I don't think Avery and I can survive months of this.

I'm not positive Avery has really survived *this.*

She hasn't moved since I walked in.

I sit on the fucking stool.

As much to be closer to her as anything.

"*Good,*" my father coos. "What a good girl."

What a bad man.

Can a good girl be the daughter of a bad man?

"What's the plan?"

Greg doesn't sound unsure anymore. Greg doesn't sound hesitant. Greg sounds like a soldier. Shit has hit the fan, and Greg is knee-jerking back to what he's best at. Stone soldiers follow orders. Stone soldiers have clear directives and they carry them out without hesitation, or guilt, or individual human conscience. They are one pebble on a mountainside of scree. They are hurled at their enemies by the omnipotent power of gravity. Death is an inevitability of life. The instruments of it do not wonder, or weep.

"If she's here," Greg voices, "the others have escaped, or they're at least fighting their way here. My men are good but," he shrugs, "shit happens. If she got past, the others can get past. And if it's you and me versus a whole contingent, we're screwed."

My father is already walking towards the door.

"Yes," he murmurs. It's his oh-so-reasonable voice again. "I agree. I think we will be traveling to Italy after all. And we might move up our timetable on that just a bit." He's pulling out his cell phone as he walks and it's such a ludicrous image, so ridiculous that it looks so natural, such an everyday moment in the midst of this *insane* moment, in the midst of *all* the insane moments that just seem to keep coming lately. My father in one of his suit jackets and a pair of khaki slacks like he's out for a lunch with his 'associates' on the weekend. My father's face, the genial one he wears when I can sense the calculations just beneath the surface, wondering how much he can squeeze from this guy, how can he manipulate this other bastard to do his bidding, at least however long he's useful, and then how will he get rid of him? All those thoughts that I could always sense, I realize, flickering behind those too calm eyes. Even when his face smiled, his eyes never really did. Always a troop of crows, fluttering behind that gaze. Always circling, always watching, always cawing out in portend to doom.

I giggle.

Mostly at my own thoughts.

Mostly in terror.

Doom.

I actually thought the word 'doom'.

It's so melodramatic.

And it's actually completely fucking appropriate, under the circumstances.

You know it's bad when 'doom' is an apt descriptor.

Fuck.

My father just glances back at me with a smile I hate because it says, 'I understand you'. And I think he does. I think he knows a whole fucking lot about giggling as you go mad.

"I'll make the arrangements," is all he says. To Greg. "Keep an eye on Catherine. Get the Old Man as stable as you can so we can get him out of here. And…" He takes a long look at Avery's hanging head, Avery's beautiful, broken body. And he says, "Assess that one. We can't afford to let her slow us down."

He leaves it at that, walks out the door, already dialing.

But the words he doesn't speak are as obvious as the ones he did and I gag on them.

If Avery is going to slow us down, then she's not coming.

My father cares so little about Avery, cares so little about *me* and how much *I* care about Avery, cares so little about *anything* really, that it's that easy for him to order her death. Just one more 'arrangement' that must be made. It doesn't even make his steps pause on the stairs. His voice is steady and without inflection as he tells someone on the other end of the phone to 'File the flight plan. I want us in the air by eight.'

Morning, I realize. Eight AM.

There are no windows in the basement and so no way to tell, but the bomb, the run, sneaking down here to this cellar…

Greg said the other gargoyles would be driving in *tomorrow.* Saturday.

So.

It's officially Friday.

Somewhere in the midst of all this insanity, the clock kicked over from PM to AM.

It's… Friday.

I sit on my stool, stupefied, as Greg takes his first lumbering step towards the 'Old Man' I've barely even glanced at since I got here. *God* himself is sitting two feet to my right, but all I noticed of him was a shock of grey hair and a lanky old body curled over itself in a chair. Just a glance. Just that one moment I walked into the cellar, bullets blazing.

Even now, I still can't be bothered to look to my right.

It's right in front of me I want to see.

It's Avery.

Still breathing, I realize, even after my ricocheting bullets. Her head is still hanging, so I still can't see her face, but her body is shaking. She's –

Crying, I realize.

Stone girl, stone *heart*, she said…

Crying.

I hear the Old Man groan and his chair scrape against the floor. They tried reasoning with him, no doubt, in the beginning. Surely they tried bullying next. Even in my one glance, I saw enough blood to know they tried breaking *him*. And when none of that worked, they tried *heartbreaking*, didn't they? Because that's what Avery is. Avery's broken beauty. Avery, the stone girl with the stone heart, *crying*.

It's *heartbreaking*.

And I giggle again because it's *Friday*.

It has been exactly one week since Avery strolled up to my rescue when my car broke down.

I'd realized then that the fairy tales I was told as a child were a lie.

That a girl in ripped jeans might be just as likely to save the day as a knight in armor.

That I might be a hell of a lot more likely to love that girl than that knight.

That it was a big, wide, wild, terrifying world.

And I was living in it.

Maybe I should have wondered then:

If *all* fairy tales are lies.

Even the ones with the girls in ripped jeans.

Maybe no one saves the day.

Maybe the bad guys *win* sometimes.

Maybe even the girl with the stone heart, gets her heart broken.

Sixteen *years* I lived a simple life with simple absolutes. Rules. Norms. Expectations.

Mostly, people did what they were told, *were* who they were told to be.

The world was small, and simple, and straightforward.

Until one *week* ago, today.

In one week I've lived more, learned more, and loved more than I did in all that time before. In one week I've lost more. But I've gained more too.

It is quite possible that in one week I have become an entirely different person, that the girl sitting here on this stool, *this* Friday, is an entirely different girl than the one that was sitting in her broken car *last*

Friday.

I start at that.

Last Friday I was petrified, sitting in my car, wondering what dangers might lurk on the dark city streets.

This Friday I'm sitting on a stool with blood splattered all around me and a killer at my back and I'm giggling.

No doubt the loss of my sanity accounts for some of that.

But in an insane world...

Maybe insanity is only sane.

I am not the same Catherine I was a week ago.

One week ago today, *that* Catherine met Avery, and everything changed.

She changed.

Maybe *this* Catherine doesn't need Avery to save her.

Maybe *this* Catherine can save *Avery.*

This Catherine watches Greg very, very carefully.

This Catherine waits.

Daryn is a librarian. Weekends are spent writing with a faithful, furry assistant and far too much coffee.

NONFICTION

Hello Queer Ones
Wendy Judith Cutler

The following piece was inspired by a prompt during our magical nonfiction workshop. It began as an epistolary and I drew from some other writings written during the workshop. It is a love letter of sorts, having spent a precious and transformative week amongst other queer writers with whom I have so deeply bonded, an experience I will never forget. At the end, I have included excerpts of some of the comments we shared with one another (in emails) after the retreat.

Here I am amongst a gathering of writers—we queer ones—to commune and collect our thoughts and goals and to express our passions onto the page. We sit in our places in the circle, created by pushing several tables together, close enough for contact yet also firmly situated in our own selves. We continue to occupy the same seat in this room during our mornings writing and sharing together, a bonding ritual of sorts, generated from the first evening we came together. Diana conjured us, summoned us to appear. The first night she reassures us that we are the ones who are supposed to be here. It is fated.

We queer writers, critical thinkers, dreamers, cultural boundary interrupters, in our particular diversities and textures, we are the voices that need to be heard, to contribute to the dialogue, the insights that are so desperately needed. We may be the very ones to articulate the moans and sighs and exaltations, to confront and celebrate, discover and disseminate. We are the hope givers, the rhythm and change makers, the seers.

I acknowledge the trepidation I felt about attending this retreat. Ambivalence and insecurities flooded my thoughts as I arrived. I wondered what I was doing here and why did I even want to attend. I craved the validation of being accepted into this utterly unique gathering of queer "emerging" writers and, at the same time, I was unsure of what I was going to find.

Community. I found community.

We are asked during our retreat workshop to write about the main purpose of our writing. "Community" is the word that comes to me—creating community. This is perhaps the most vital aspect of what I am writing about. That without other folks, communing with others in whatever way you are, you're not doing the work that needs to be done. We're doing some of it here, amongst one another, our bodies on our chairs in this room, exchanging breaths, exhale, inhale, our fingers tapping on the keys or sliding our pens across the pages. This is so important to me and I would not be able to exist without it, without you and your ancestors and all of those you touch. We are a humongous circle of energies, bringing who we are into connection, communication, community.

And I know that the Internet is a resource (I get it), but it doesn't take the place of THIS. I am a junkie for THIS. I feel that we are supposed to be doing THIS. Here and now and where we now live. And it is messy and it hurts, but I also know that I feel accepted here, that my heart feels open, more sometimes than others, but still open. I feel that life is somewhat worth living, yes, definitely worth living, to be able to feel alive in this moment, even as we are all tapping away on our screens or gliding our pens across the pages.

I reflect upon the "queerness" of this, our coming together as queer-identified people that I am convinced is such an immense part of the magic of our being together. This stunning mixture—of our genders, sexualities, racial, ethnic, class, generational identities—creates such a rich and potent cauldron. From this diversity, combined with the astute and incisive intelligence, insights and perceptions that we each bring during our discussions, interactions and critiques, emerges a rare kind of richness and depth of feeling that is so foundational to the hearts, minds and spirits we share within this brief week of being and coming together.

This is the thing—we must feel part of something so that we can feel wholly accepted, which is utterly different from being merely tolerat-ed. Only then can we truly accept ourselves. When we share who we really are, our pains and pleasures, the fullness of our experiences and expres-sions, our creativity and concerns, we are being truly alive. I hope that we continue to feel this kind of opening, even if not everyone in this room feels this at this exact moment. I am being moved and you are moving me and I am part of this. This is the essence of collectivity, of collaboration and of truly creating community with one another.

To have hope in times of despair is the very thing we all need, every single one of us. Queers, people of colour, the disenfranchised and the invisible—those of us on the margins, which is actually the majority of us, though we are led to believe differently—we are the ones who are creating the stories and leading the struggles and calling out the contra-dictions and working to save our planet and world from homogenization and a bleak and disheartening future.

The lesbian feminist revolutionaries of the seventies inspired me to see the reasons for massive, transformational social, political and personal change. Feminists could not have existed without the models of protest and challenge that came before. The civil rights movement for racial and economic equality (because poverty was and is also a ma-jor concern) spawned other liberation movements including those for women's liberation, Latino/a rights, native rights, disability rights, welfare rights, prisoner rights, disability rights and, of course, the gay, lesbian, queer, trans and now LGBTQ+ movements. My own life has been lived in the cauldron of these vibrant and inspirational movements for change that followed and flowed throughout the decades since I was born.

Where am I from, I am asked. Sort of from here. I return to my birthplace, this city of angels, from which I so desperately needed to es-cape. After high school, moving northward to attend university in Berke-ley—I often credit this as the most significant decision I ever made in my life—entering into the tumultuous and frenzied anti-war movement filled with demonstrations, arrests and radical politics. Then, I journeyed across the continent for a brief detour to the middle of Vermont to attend a wildly progressive and permissive college and my introduction to feminism, sex with boys and marijuana. Then my return to the Berkeley campus into the radical criminology department, which focused on the crimes of racism, sexism and imperialism. While critiquing the (unjust) criminal justice system, I became part of an anti-rape collective, a member of a socialist-feminist women's union and experienced the beautiful and sometimes painful ramifications of coming out as a lesbian and entering into my first lesbian relationship. After heartbreak and graduation, I moved two hours south to enter an interdisciplinary graduate program in Santa Cruz, in the redwoods by the sea. Later, moving northward to Oregon and the city of roses and bridges with another lover, after my favourite (gay) professor was refused tenure and forced to leave the university. After a few years, with more heartbreak and loss than I'd ever experienced, leaving her and traveling back and forth again, to Santa Cruz and then Oakland and commuting to another graduate program in San Francisco that I completed as I entered into a long-distance relationship (between Oakland and Portland). And, with my master's degree, returning to Portland to live with my lovergirl-life partner. Then, finally, immigrating together to another country on the island paradise of our dreams in British Columbia.

We are all doing what we are doing because other brave, courageous and regular folks have resisted, spoken out, gathered with others, protested or just said "no." They had the resilience to continue to live their lives, show up, take stands and feel that they were part of something larger, more vast than themselves. My life, and the lives of so many of us, would not be the same if we hadn't had these incredible models who came before us.

I, for one, want always to honour our ancestors, our mentors and our activists and know that every day, each moment, we have the opportunity, the possibilities to bring these life-robbing systems down and listen to and learn from those who can show us other ways. Are we listening?

I hear Audre Lorde's voice, that is as potent and relevant as it was when she voiced it forty years ago, in a talk she gave at the Modern Lan-

guage Association's "Lesbian and Literature
Panel":

What are the words you do not yet have? What do you need to say? What are
the tyrannies you swallow day by day and attempt to make your own, until
you will sicken and die of them, still in silence?...The fact that we are here
and that I speak these words is an attempt to break that silence and bridge
some of the differ ences between us, for it is not difference which immobiliz-
es us, but silence. And there are so many silences to be broken.

Today, in my black buddha-covered book, I find words I copied from last
December 2016's *Lambda Literary Review* by Justin Torres, a past Lambda
Literary Fellow:

To my mind, queer literature is about the respect of difference, not the se-
ductive respectability of sameness. To my mind, queerness has always been
about identification and solidarity with the objected and the devalued, the
tossed off. Queernesss has always been attracted to the forbidden.

What we are doing here, and at our desks and in our offices and at our
workplaces and workshops and classes and meetings and gatherings and
demonstrations and protests and homes and cafes and bars and beds, is
vital to sustaining and nurturing queer voices. I pledge to remember each
one of you and the exquisite mixture of just the perfect ones to create our
magical, meaningful, enriching, inspirational queer nonfiction writing circle. We are witnessing one another and, as queer writers, we are breaking
the silence by doing what we are doing.

     This is the power of the circle, that we are all here together, open,
opening, receiving, witnessing. I hope we can hold this connection within
and continue to move it out into our worlds, into other worlds, directly,
fervently, passionately. This is our gift, our artistry, our responseability, our
inheritance as the queer writers that we are.

Messages we shared with each other after the retreat:

We gave each other so much. And I am grateful.

Back to civilization, and it is NOT even remotely close to the comfort and sophistication of being around you all. So much love—let's keep it going year round.

I feel like I have a newfound confidence and sense of purpose that I would not have without you all. I'm here for you and I know you're there for me.

I have so much regular life stuff to catch up on and it is all so boring compared to being with our group. I miss you guys. What a strange yet awesome thing to be together all day, every day.

Just sending some love out. And just generally missing our 9am to noon magic. xoxox

So much busy & not enough "comfort and sophistication" of you all! I'm also happy to keep sharing work, inspiration and encouragement.

As I sit here and write, I can literally feel you all around me.

I hope you all are doing well. Miss you more than you could ever know.

But now, at least, I have last week, to remind me of what's possible, that my voice is not like anyone else's, and that our stories need telling.

THANK YOU SO MUCH. Also, send me your shit! I want to read it and give you feedback.

I still hear your voices and feel your support here. Missing you all very much.

I've been reflecting a lot and I am just so thankful for the space that we shared. Community often looks and feels different than I expect it to. Thank you for being brave queer folk.

I am missing EACH AND EVERY ONE OF YOU! So much love and inspiration from you. With so much love, longing and queerness.

Notes

Audre Lorde. "The Transformation of Silence into Language and Action." *Sister Outsider: Essays and Speeches by Audre Lorde.* New York: Crossing Press, 1984.

Justin Torres. "Don't Get Used To It: Queer Literature in a Time of Triumph." *Emerge: 2015 Lambda Literary Fellows Anthology* (Volume 1), 2016.

Wendy Judith Cutler is a radical teacher, queer writer and lesbian feminist activist. She was born in Los Angeles, educated in the Bay Area, taught writing and women's studies in Oregon and now resides on Salt Spring Island, the unceded territory of the Coast Salish peoples. She is co-author of Writing Alone Together: Journalling in a Circle of Women for Creativity, Compassion and Connection. Her essay, co-written with Corrie Hope Furst, her life partner, "Crossing Borders: A Lesbian Immigration Story in Two Voices," is published in the anthology Breaking Boundaries: LGBTQ2 Writers Coming Out and Into Canada. She is currently at work on Memoir of An Undutiful Daughter: Lesbian Feminist Transformation in the 1970s.

Tressie, Dolores, and Me: A Woman's Search for Family
an excerpt
Lourdes Dolores Follins

Chapter 1: The Beginning

This book technically has three beginnings, three start dates. The first
beginning is when I was 22 years old and living at home with my parents after graduating from college. I can't remember if it's because I'm a
Cancerian and we like history and solving puzzles and care deeply about
all matters related to family-or because of some random conversation with
my mother, but it was then that that I got the bright idea of researching
my family tree. When I asked my mother about her history, she retorted,
"I don't *have* any history," and went back to whatever she was doing when
I interrupted her. I was outraged! "We *all* have history; sometimes we just
don't know it!" I protested, as if she was talking about me.... But...she *was*
talking about me. She was talking about *us*. She was saying that we, our
family, had *no* history, came from *nowhere*, did *nothing* of import, and left
no mark on the world. We did not exist and we were never here. We were
less than dust. For some reason, that bothered me and stuck in my craw....

This book also began the day my mother died on June 18th, 2014.
Five days earlier, my mother had a hysterectomy. On June 12th, 2014, at
11:16 pm, my mother sent me this odd, cryptic text: "Please call me before
10 Am today (Friday) MoM." Since I did not see her text until the next
morning, that was when I called her.

"Hi, Ma! What's going on?" With great nonchalance, my mother
said that she was having surgery that day. Alarmed, I asked, "What kind of
surgery?!"

"Oh, a hysterectomy...."

"A hysterectomy?! Why are you having a hysterectomy??!"

Even more nonchalantly, my mother replied, "Oh, I have some fibroids...." You would have thought she was having a hangnail removed! So, I tried to respond with sangfroid:

"Oh, okay.... Do you want me to be there?"

"Oh...if you want."

I had had enough of trying to be composed after having just awakened at 7:30am and was about to lose my shit. Instead of following my usual morning routine of eating breakfast and having some water that day, when I saw my mother's text, I sat up and called my mother. So, I was a bit cranky and the fact that my mother was being her usual diva self did not make the conversation go smoothly. "Ma, do you want me there or not?! If you want me there, I'll be there! Just let me know."

Pregnant pause.

"Ok, you can be there."

So, I took the day off from work and ran to the Richmond University Medical Center to be there for my 64-year-old mother's hysterectomy later that day. She had the surgery, was discharged in two days, and died five days after her surgery. At home. On the floor. In my parents' bedroom.

The third beginning of this book was when my grandmother, Ethel "Tressie" Dargan Warren, came North for the second and final time in 1949. She was one of the millions of Black Americans who left the South between 1910 and 1970 in search of better economic opportunities and fleeing domestic terrorism during the Great Migration. Pregnant with my mother, Dolores, Tressie travelled to New York City from Darlington, South Carolina with two of her four children. Unlike most women who made the same migration, Tressie left behind her parents, her first two children, and her second husband, Henry. However, within three years of her arrival, Ethel gave birth to her last child, became ill with tuberculosis, and her three youngest children were placed in foster care. Tressie was a working-class Black woman with a 4th grade education and from what I could find, she was all alone in New York City. Tressie never regained custody of her children, but miraculously maintained relationships with her six children.

This book is about Tressie and Dolores: who they were, how they were shaped by their surroundings and circumstances, and how they managed to salvage a relationship despite the odds. The impetus for this book is the realization that the woman that I called "Mom" was so much more than my mother. Unfortunately, I realized this after she died as I went through, organized, and pored over her belongings as the administrator of her estate. The boxes of photographs that my mother had hoarded for decades revealed that she had been a beautiful, playful child with an easy, wide smile. It was during interviews with family members that I learned that my mother had always wanted to be a nurse and that she enjoyed climbing up on top of the roof with her little tool belt to help her foster father, Claude, fix it. I remembered that my mother had told me that, as a child, she spent *hours* at the cinema, mesmerized by the sights and sounds, and then at supper, proudly regaled her family with all that she saw. I learned from my dad and an uncle that she blossomed into a self-sufficient young woman who bristled at the fact that her foster mother, Gladys, borrowed and wore her clothes without her permission. Letters that had long been tucked away revealed that two months before I was born, she was heartbroken and devastated to learn that my biological father, her husband, never wanted children.

I began writing this book so that I could understand who my mother was and to fulfill my need for closure that I assumed her sudden death had robbed me of achieving. However, the more I pieced together what I had discovered about my mother, the more I realized that I had to re-examine all that I had discovered about my grandmother Tressie so many years ago. I also began to recognize that there had been what psychotherapists refer to as a 'parallel process' all along. Despite the strain and emotional disconnection, as an adult daughter I was increasingly determined to 'do right' by my mother, the same way that she was always determined to 'do right' by her mother. This meant that when our mothers were mentally or physically ill, we stepped forward to care for them, even as they sat silent and glum. That meant believing very deep in our marrow that we were as responsible for our mothers' wellbeing in their twilight years as much as they were responsible for us in our childhood. We two daughters struggled until our mothers' very end to take care of them in ways that they may not have had the emotional capacity to take care of us. This book is about the ways in which two Black working-class women came to create and maintain a mother-daughter relationship when it would have been much easier to let go and walk away. It's also about my search for my family in the form of my mother and the grandmother who had the most impact on my physical, emotional, and spiritual development, even though I barely knew her.

Chapter 2: Tracing Our Roots

How do you research and accurately portray the lives and perspectives of two Black women whose ancestors were enslaved in the United States and before 1865 whose first names were only found on Bills of Sales or plantation inventories? Additionally, how do you write about the lives of two women who were literally separated by the State because of racism, classism, and misogynoir, through the removal and placement of children into foster care? To complicate matters further, how do you locate in history and describe the experiences of a Black working-class woman who did not leave a paper trail, who left no legible mark on this earth besides her children? Finally, how do you learn and write about the lives of two people you barely knew—one quite literally (my grandmother) and the other, figuratively (my mother)? The answers to these questions have become evident over the last 25 years.

    Although I had never known anyone who had researched their family history, it made sense to ask my mother to tell me anything and everything she knew or could recall about her family. Before I began this research, there was never a mention of anything from the past—hers, mine, or ours—before we moved in with my stepfather, Harold, and his four sons. So, being my mother's child, I meticulously typed up a four-page list of 43 questions on my word processor and was prepared to treat our 'interview' like those I had with children and their families in my first-year social work field placement. I still have the list of questions, which was appropriately titled, "My Mother's Story" and under the title it presciently states that "the purpose of the interview" was "to document my mother's life thus far and to gain a better understanding of what it was like and is like to be her. This information may become either and essay or part of a book; it is yet to be determined."

One of the first challenges was sorting out what she knew about her foster family and had pieced together about her biological family. I was initially armed with pen and paper, but eventually switched to pencil because I quickly realized that people's memories seem to contract and expand the more they talk about the past. As the words alternately tripped and flowed out of my mother's mouth, I scribbled down as much as I could as her memories seemed to unfold before us. For the first time, I learned about histories of cancer, alcoholism, numerous violent and odd deaths, and infertility as well as the fact that my mother had several biological siblings and cousins I had never heard of nor met! I was transfixed and wanted to know more about these people, my people. Unfortunately, there weren't many of these kinds of conversations, for my mother worked full-time and my graduate studies were soon under way.

Armed with the sundry bits of information my mother gave me and without internet access, I somehow ended up at the New York City branch of the National Archives. I cannot remember how many days or hours I spent there, but I remember sitting in quiet, dimly-lit rooms, searching for the familiar and mostly unfamiliar names of my ancestors, and poring over rolls and rolls of United States Census schedules on microfilm. After many sojourns to the National Archives, I returned home, shared what I found with my mother and peppered her with even more questions about her biological family. At some point, I got the sense that her interest had waned and equally important, that my mother seemed uncomfortable talking about her past and the two branches of her family—foster and biological. So, I stopped asking questions and continued with my quest for people with first names and surnames that were unfamiliar yet comforting to me: Antney Dargan, Decatur ("Detoya") Williams, Sylvia Govan, Traxler Dargan, Willie Mae ("Squirrel"), and Ethel Sams Dargan.

The Mother-Daughter Genealogy Trip: 1999

Over the next seven years, my interest in and enthusiasm for this quest waxed and waned, competing with living an actively single Black queer girl's life in New York City, completing a master's degree, working as a social worker, and entering a doctoral program for clinical social work. Intermittently, I visited the New York City branch of the National Archives and managed to trace my ancestry back to 1838 on my mother's maternal side of her family, the Dargans, and back to 1834 on my mother's paternal side of her family, the Warrens. But in 1999, I asked my mother if she wanted to take "a mother-daughter genealogy trip" to Darlington, South Carolina where both of her parents were from, to see what else we could learn together. Much to my surprise and delight, my mother was interested and even excited! Typically, my mother had an almost studied calmness about her and did not get excited about many things, so to see her smile broadly, with a twinkle in her eye was promising. In May 1999, just before my 30th and my mother's 50th birthday we travelled to Darlington to see what we could find. Darlington County is in the northeastern part of South Carolina and the area was inhabited by the Pee Dee indigenous people before it was 'settled' in the mid-1700s by Welsh, Scotch-Irish, and English men and their families.

I do not recall much of the trip to and in Darlington, but I shared a motel room at the Days Inn in Florence, South Carolina with my mother. That was when I discovered that she snored so loudly that it sounded like she was sawing down trees and even worse to me, that she slept with the television on all night. Our first night there, I tried to turn off the TV when I was ready to go to sleep. My mother appeared to be asleep, but she promptly awakened, like a hibernating bear who was poked with a stick. The television remained on and I eventually passed out and fell asleep. The next day, I tried to broach these subjects gently:

"Ma...do you know that you snore?"

"Yeah...." She sounded haughty.

"Is there anything you can *do* about it?"

"No."

"Hmmm....Well, why do you sleep with the TV on?"

"Because I'm *watching* it."

"Ma, you're sleeping! The TV's watching you!"

"Well, I start out watching TV and then I fall asleep...but I wake up from time to time."

"But then...you never fall completely asleep?"

"No."

Puzzled, I asked, "Why?"

"Because I don't like falling deep asleep."

Feeling as if I was speaking with a small child who was wearing my patience thin, I asked, "But *why??*"

My mother shook her head and added, "I don't want to miss anything." I was thoroughly confused; my mother, a 49-year-old psychiatric nurse, was telling me that she purposefully prohibited herself from getting a full night's sleep because she did not want to "miss anything". This made no sense to me at the time. In retrospect, as a psychotherapist and sexual assault survivor, I wondered what would make a woman purposefully deprive herself of the physiological need to sleep deeply and fully. Had my mother been molested a child? Was there some other unresolved childhood trauma that made her afraid to fall "deep asleep" or was it simply that my mother viewed the world as it was portrayed in television reruns from the 1960s, black and white movies from the 1950s, and documentaries as simply too riveting to look away? Unfortunately, I will never know my mother's 'real' reasons for depriving herself of sleep, but it was a way of being that persisted until the day she died.

Our mother-daughter genealogy trip was also challenging for me because although it was the first time I had gone to Darlington as an adult. We briefly lived there when I was three years old—I immediately connected with stereotypical Southern mannerisms and my mother did not. Little things like saying "Hello" and "Good morning" to people you do not know just because they are fellow humans sharing your space and moving slower because there is no need to rush anywhere intuitively felt right to me. Once I said, "Good morning" in response to a white man who walked by my mother and me.

"Did you know him?" my mother blurted out. Nonplussed, I paused because I didn't understand the question or why my mother asked it.

I replied, "No."

"So, why did you say, 'Good morning' to that man?" she asked with skepticism.

Baffled, I responded, "Because he said, '*Good morning*'!" She still didn't understand. Even though my mother was *conceived* in the South, she was a slightly guarded and reserved Northerner. I, who was born up North and two generations removed, was more naturally drawn to and appreciative of Southern mannerisms, cuisine, sayings, and gestures than my mother. Seeing this tendency in my mother made me dislike her a little bit more than I already did and at various times during our trip, I found myself rolling my eyes or simply ignoring her.

Despite these unpleasant discoveries about my mother, there were many moments during our trip that were eye-opening in positive ways. While I had always known that my mother enjoyed puzzles and mysteries, seeing her face light up as the librarian at the Darlington Public Library showed us more ways to find out information about our ancestors was priceless! When the librarian informed us that over several years, the local historical society had searched for, surveyed and documented the former and old cemeteries of formerly enslaved Blacks in the county. Neither my mother or I had known about or expected this and when we heard this, we turned to each other like two little girls who found out that the Easter Bunny who left coins under our pillows was real!

There was also that time at the South Carolina branch of the National Archives in Columbia, SC when we searched for and found the 1924 death certificate of my mother's great-grandmother Polly Warren and the 1940 death certificate of my mother's grandmother, Ethel Dargan. As we both peered that our female ancestors' occupations at the time of their death ("domestic") and what was written down as the causes of their deaths, my mother looked both bemused and intrigued, while I was both confused and annoyed. Although she was a psychiatric nurse, my mother was very well-versed in medical terms and the names of many illnesses having been both an avid learner of medicine and diagnoses as well as a cardiac patient for most of her life. So, when she read that the "principal cause of death" was "mitral stenosis" for my great-grandmother Ethel, my mother nodded and looked pensive.

"Mitral stenosis? What's that?" I asked. I was a bit of an undercover medical geek, but had never heard that diagnosis before. I knew the word "mitral" was related to the mitral value because my mother had had her mitral value replaced 12 years earlier. But "stenosis" was a new word for me.

"Mitral stenosis? It's a narrowing of the mitral value," my mother replied, as she continued to peer at the death certificate. She said it as if she was telling me what day of the week it was.

"Okay...so, how can someone die from it?" I was slightly annoyed because I didn't think that was an answer.

"Well.... If the mitral value narrows, it prevents blood from flowing through the heart properly. And if the blood cannot flow through the heart in the right direction, it gets backed up and can lead to heart failure."

"Oh!" This sounded like a long, slow, and potentially painful process. My great-grandmother Ethel was only 56 when she died and according to the death certificate, she had had mitral stenosis for about a year. My mother was not fazed by this in the least and continued to read every line, eagerly trying to decipher every curlicue on the documents.

Lourdes Dolores Follins is a Black femme writer who comes from a long line of badass survivors and working-class strivers. She is also a first-generation college graduate and a Yoruba/Lukumi priest of Ogun.

Paul

Dr. Jonathan P. Higgins

"Oh. Well I am deeply flattered, but you're not my type."

Type. A word that I learned to become deeply connected to. It was a word that I heard often since the first time I logged on to XY.com, a place where I thought my queer Black body would find solace in a world that had always categorized my existence. And this wouldn't be the first time that I was body slammed into a metaphorical box.

There was the one time at Rage in West Hollywood when I walked over to the cute Latinx guy standing on the wall and asked him to dance and he laughed in my face. That one time when I did ask a guy to dance down at Ripples in San Diego and when I asked him for his number, he gently chuckled and said, "you know, I don't really date big guys." Let us not forget the one time I cried myself to sleep after leaving Oasis Night-club in Upland, CA because a guy walked past me to go ask my friend to dance.

Denunciation in rare form. I was in fact a type, the type of queer Black man that other cis-normative men had learned to fear.

The rejection I faced on the boulevard of broken dreams wasn't unusual. Desperate. Thirsty, miserable. All things men had used to describe me. All the words I had learned to internalize. All words I to describe the yearning I had for Paul. Because l loved Paul. Because I wanted and I needed Paul.

Wait.

I loved the idea of Paul. I wanted something that Paul could never give me.

I could never understand him. Paul was a trained magician. Here today, gone today. Never in one place for to long. His light brown eyes, smooth voice, caramel brown skin and scent of Michael Jordan cologne kept people enamored. But it also kept people hurt. IIis mother. His first wife. His first daughter. My Mother. My brother. Me.

Paul was a master manipulator who kept everyone on long leash of pain and sadness.So close, but distant. A master illusionist. Always fine tuning the master of his craft.

Paul 's magic found my mother in 1984 in a roller rink in Inglewood, CA. A place where all young Black Jehovah Witnesses would congregate on the weekends. After a year of what my mother said was "courtship," Paul and my Mother were married and expecting a young baby boy. Five years later, they would be divorced leaving my mother to take care of her then 5 year old son Jonathan, and her then three year old son, Justin.

One Saturday afternoon, I could hear my mother from the kitchen yelling for my brother to hurry up and pack. "Where is your shoes Justin? You always do this. Waiting to the last damn minute to do what I asked you to do." I stood looking outside the dusty black screen door hoping and waiting to hear the sound of a classic porche come up the street and turn the corner. It had been almost three years since the divorce and my brother and I were elated with the idea that Paul was finally reaching out after spending 2 years in county jail. He called us here and there to tell us what movie he was going to be in. Told us what celebrity he was hanging out with and what celebrities we would get to meet once we got over to his house. Paul told us a lot of things that day including that he would be there around 3:00pm pacific standard time.

The thing is he never did.

Paul 's master skill was lying. He had lied to my mother for several years about the affair and now I was in for the best show in town. "I had car problems. I forgot I had an audition. I didn't have enough money for gas." You would have thought that him and rumpelstiltskin went to same art school. "Could sell you back your own underwear," my mom would often say about him.

Every year up to my 15th birthday I learned to expect a lie from him. Lies that often left me desperate for affection. Lies that left me thirsting to be loved but most, miserably broken.

Paul was the man I was always looking for. Paul would be the first man to break my heart.

I could never comprehend how someone could use the term "love" so carelessly. But as I got older, I began to understand that the same man who said he loved me left physical scars on my mother. Drove her nearly insane to a point where she spent a weekend in a psych ward. Left my mother to raise two Black men in a world much like the wild safaris of Africa. Except, he would always be the hunter and the people he loved were the game. If that were love, I would never comprehend its true meaning.

I would ask my mother ritually why Paul could never keep his words. My mother would always reply that hurt people hurt people, but that response never seemed to set well with me. The truth of the matter was that Paul wasn't good with handling delicate things.

He would break my mother and then proceed to break me. I was the kid that Paul did not want. I am the child that Paul never wanted. I am that overly feminine, fat, cis-gendered queer Black man that the queer community does not want. But I have always wanted and needed someone to want me, even if it meant it being for just five minutes. I wanted someone to love me the way Paul never could.

Dr. Jonathan P. Higgins is a speaker, educator and thought leader.

With over ten years of experience in education, social justice and grassroots movements, Dr. Higgins is focused on public speaking and working with the media on issues centered on people of color, LGBTQ storytelling and marginalized communities. His work has been included on Blavity, The Root, Efniks, Wear Your Voice and Talkspace. Dr. Higgins serves as Campus Pride's Curriculum Educator, is a Lambda Literary writing fellow and a regular contributor to SOULE.

The Trouble with Muffin
an excerpt
Evan James

Hugh's faltering confidence left him pacing his room at the lodge. He thought back to the year previous, when, in a deep creative depression (his last film, the original comedy *A Whole Lot of Fun*, had been a total flop), he had gotten stoned and ordered a cleansing diet system called Inconsequent Design online. During that week of fasting, rocked by splitting headaches, all-too brief moments of clarity, and gassy interludes, Hugh also found a manila envelope containing only his address—no name—in the mailbox. Inside was a book by P.J. Snodhurst, a sloppy, early-period slapstick comedy about birds, people, and synchronicity called *Flock of Reasons*.

Why had it come? Had it been a special offer included with Inconsequent Design? He never found out, but so intrigued and giggly was he over *Flock of Reasons* that he began reading all the Snodhurst he could, simultaneously flushing toxins from his system: a hilarious series of novels about a bumbling aristocratic party boy and his problem-solving servant, Rupert (*Cheers, Rupert; Rather Impressive, Rupert; Rupert Rides Again*); *Three Times Removed,* the first of his side-splitting works about unbelievably evil step-cousins; and, finally, *Precious Umbrage*, a farce about several wealthy young Edwardians summering at an idyllic manor in the English countryside and acting all lovey-dovey. It was in the middle of this book, and on the final day of his cleanse, that Hugh, aching with laughter, began to see cinematic visions as he read. He felt some higher power lifting him from the nest of ice-cream sandwich wrappers on his couch, leading him marionette-like to the shower, and plopping him down again at his desk, where he began to adapt *Precious Umbrage* for the screen.

He had been so placidly happy then, ravished by inspiration.

Financing, location scouting, and the assembling of cast and crew had gone smoothly. He had felt confident. There were still chinks in his armor, though, and one of these had been pierced that morning. Dazed by the possibility that his adaptation might be a disaster after all—and what was worse, an insult to the spirit of Snodhurst—he stood at the window, staring out at the sunlit perfection of the grounds.

A knock came at the door. Hugh turned and, having blinked a few times, recognized in the snappily dressed woman who entered his Assistant Director, Dawn Hayward. She, too, appeared as though she hadn't slept a wink.

"Hugh," she cried, "we're in serious trouble."

Hugh nodded dully. "Uh, I know, Dawn. I know."

"Ah, you already know, then."

"I've been, like, knowing about it all morning."

"What! So you knew about it before I did?"

"God, Dawn, I'm the director. I know things."

"Why didn't you tell me? Damage control, Hugh."

"Nothing personal, Dawn, but, like, I like to deal with this kind of damage on my own." Hugh, eyes bloodshot, his hair a mess, dressed in white pajamas with a multi-colored kitten head pattern, did not at that moment look like the kind of person who could "deal with" damage of any kind.

"On your own, Hugh?" Dawn laughed. "I think you might be in over your head on this one."

"Maybe," he said, having considered the point. "But this is my baby, Dawn. It's, like, my project. My baby project. And I feel personally bummed about it, like Snodhurst is looking down on me and I'm blowing it."

"Baby project? What are you talking about?"

"Uh, I'm talking about the scene where Dashiell jumps out of the hay pile and proposes to Holly. Duh. Earth to Dawn."

As frequently happened when she tried to have a logical conversation with Hugh, Dawn experienced a swimming sensation in the head.

"Then you haven't heard. Hugh, that haystack fiasco was so twelve hours ago. Something far worse has happened. This morning, while doing her morning elocution exercises out on the lawn, Irene kicked Muffin in a fit of rage."

"Ech! And the end of shooting is scheduled for this week!" cried Hugh, falling back on the bed, his arms outstretched.

"What has that got to do with it?" demanded Dawn.

"What has that got to do with it? Only, like, everything. Less than one week left, and my big romantic barn scene is a bust. The dialogue is a ludicrous mockery, my rewrite attempts are a disaster, and—"

"Queen, please! Will you stop thinking about barnyard romance for one minute? There's not going to *be* a barn scene, because your leading man has, '*like*,' gone on *strike*. Apparently this Muffin-kicking incident worked his last nerve, and he's declared actor war on Irene. He called her an 'enemy of on-set animal rights,' told her that Muffin earned more money as a performer than she ever would, and has started a petition for Susan-Anne to replace her."

"You mean the stunt-double-slash-animal-handler?"

"Yes, that. This has been going on since day one, Hugh. Graham thinks Susan-Anne is funnier than Irene, and then the fact that she always has Muffin around—well, Graham is *obsessed* with small hybrid dogs. I thought it would stay on the level of a mutual love for animals, but now they're founding some sort of professional organization that protects the rights of animals in show business. So, as you can see, Irene kicking Muffin only strengthens the Graham and Susan-Anne alliance. And that is an unholy alliance indeed."

"Obsessed with small dogs, huh?" said Hugh, who had stopped listening after that, intrigued by the dog part and confused by the rest. "Maybe that's it. Maybe Graham is gay. Whoa. Maybe I could introduce that as a kind of metatextual wink into the barn scene..."

Conscious of two eyes trying to burn holes through his kitten pajamas, he came to himself with a start.

"Uh, I mean, that's super lame! Kicking a harmless Peek-A-Pom like that. Not cool. I'll have a word with Graham. If he thinks he can run around set like a tyrant, like, accosting little animals—"

"Hugh!"

Hugh paused. Dawn appeared to be upset by something, but he couldn't imagine what. It seemed that in this last outburst he had struck just the right note—Take Charge, Get It Done, that sort of thing.

"Huh?"

"*Irene* kicked the dog."

"Oh. Irene?"

"*Yes!*" she cried. "And Graham loves that little gargoyle, apparently, as much as he loves the comic stylings of its master. The point is, what the hell are we going to do about it?"

Hugh ruminated. "Should we smoke pot?"

Dawn made a strangling gesture with her hands, searching for words scathing enough to burn through Hugh's medicinal haze. Just then, however, the door opened and a young man came in, his face looking for all the world like a disgruntled hotel worker's who received a request from Room 15 for strangulation and scathing words and came as fast as he could.

A handsome lad, Graham wore his sandy locks stuffed beneath a red baseball cap, all of that further hidden beneath the hood of a grey sweatshirt. Hugh had admired the comic actor's pretty green eyes during casting. Just now, however, they set upon Hugh and narrowed into angry slits. Hugh was disturbed, but preoccupied still with the idea that Graham might be struggling with his sexuality, and that it might be affecting his performance in the barn scene.

To ease a tense moment, Hugh said:

"Graham, is there anything you'd like to, like, tell us?"

The actor laughed bitterly. "Go to hell, Hugh."

"Whoa. What do you imagine hell would be like, Graham? Not full of male bodybuilders, I'll bet."

"Cut the crap, Hugh. Dawn tells me that if I don't make nice-nice with Irene and stay away from Susan-Anne that you'll report Muffin to the

Dog Actors Guild."

"I will?" said Hugh, turning to Dawn.

The Assistant Director grumbled. "Hugh, you know perfectly well that Muffin is threatening to derail this production, and that he's already on probation after being fired from Season Four of *Workin' Folks*."

"Well, yeah," said Hugh. "That sounds true. How about it, Gay-ram?"

Graham crossed his arms testily. "Muffin did *not* bite Irene during her elocution exercises this morning! She's *lying*, Hugh. She's psycho, to-tally unsympathetic to small animals, and yesterday she told me that comedy is for 'poor people.' Her publicist's assistant told me that she's only doing this to salvage her image after the whole thing with her stabbing Mark Tish on the set of *S Is for Serious*."

"Can we forget about stabbings for one second?" snapped Dawn. "We have a practical issue to deal with. Hugh, I've explained to Graham that while we naturally can't force him to be nice to Irene, we can demand that he fulfill the rest of his contract by jumping out of that hay pile and proposing to her. And that *despite* his threats, we have *no* intention of standing by while he petitions for an outrageous personnel change. Su-san-Anne, multi-talented as she may be, is *not* a real actress. She's nothing but an aimless athletic hireling and a handler of toothy gremlin-dogs."

"She *is* a real actress!" bellowed Graham. "She's just biding her time with stunt doubling, animal handling, and modeling while she builds up her improv, writing, and acting portfolios. It's people like you, who pigeonhole her and refuse to let her talents shine—"

"Oh, please," said Dawn. "That dog is a better actor than she'll ever be, even if he bit Misty Sinclaire during that three-episode guest appearance on *Workin' Folks*—"

"That was *two years ago*," said Graham. "Muffin's on medication now and—"

"Graham, you can argue this nonsense into the ground, but—"

"I'm *not* arguing. I'm just saying that if Muffin and Susan-Anne go, I go, even if I have to break contract and spend the rest of my days rotting away in some garret."

"Gay-ret?" said Hugh, who had been standing by the door, flipping through a copy of the script and trying to concentrate on the barn scene. "What gay-ret?"

"Any garret, Hugh!"

"Graham, please, listen to me," said Dawn.

Hugh realized that an outrageous amount of conversation unrelated to moonlit barns was taking place, and furrowed his brow accordingly. He had not expected these unannounced guests to barge into his room, to get all worked up over Irenes and Muffins and Susan-Annes while he was trying to nurse a heavy creative despair over five lines of dialogue. Both his Assistant Director and his leading man appeared to have a lot of loud, unpleasant, overlapping things to say to one another. He looked longingly past them, out the window at the splendid light, the trees swaying in the wind.

A quiet twist of the door handle behind him, then, and it was done. He slipped into the hall and down the stairs, limping gaily out into the sunlight.

Evan James' work has appeared in Oxford American, The Iowa Review, Travel +
Leisure, The Sun, The New York Observer, and elsewhere. He attended the Iowa
Writers' Workshop. He lives in New York.

Peta and the AIDS Crisis Revisitation
Theodore Kerr

Dedication: No gets HIV alone, no one should have to deal with it alone. This piece is dedicated to everyone who already knows this, and everyone who can understand this. So, it is dedicated to all of you.

In the photo, on the right side, a sister's hand cradles the top of her niece's head, covering one ear, and drawing a shoulder close. The two look forward, eyelids soft. The niece's left hand is on the hospital bed railing where her uncle, David Kirby, lays; his eyes open, looking out, above and beyond. David's father swaddles his son's head and elbow with his hands, meaty; his eyes, closed; nose, gentle against his son's forehead. Both David and his father wear watches. Above them, a painted hand beckons forward, the rest of the body cut off by a photographer's eye. To the left, another hand, body unseen, holds David's wrist.

The image, "David Kirby on his deathbed, Ohio, 1990," was taken by Therese Frare the spring that David died of complications related to AIDS. Months after, the picture was published in *Life Magazine*. Two years later, it was used for what became an infamous Benetton clothing ad. The photograph provides an important and familiar narrative—a frail young man, dying needlessly before his time. And in that, the picture also contains details and absences that speak to stories and dynamics of the ongoing AIDS crisis largely untold, teetering on the precipice of being lost.

The hand on David's wrist belongs to Peta, who, the day the photo was taken, invited Therese, a photography student at the time doing a project on AIDS, to follow as Peta did their rounds as caregiver at the hospice. Therese stayed in the hallway as Peta went in to check on David, a friend, who was near his final days. Therese had met David once before and he had given her his permission to be photographed. As Peta visited with David, David's mother invited Therese into the room, asking her to take photos of what could be their last moments all together. On Therese's contact sheets from that day, which you can view online, Peta's whole body can be seen: tall, with long hair pulled back, wearing a black leather jacket, a comb peeking out of a back pocket of light blue jeans. In Peta, we meet a caregiver from the the Pine Ridge Indian Reserve, living with HIV, who, as Therese recalls, "rode the line between genders." After David died, the Kirbys made a commitment to care for Peta as death approached, and Therese continued to photograph. In one image we find Peta in a wheelchair, looking down, hair in braids. David's parents standing behind, the sheen of Peta's silky robe midnight against the Kirbys' matte white cotton stomachs.

Recently a short web documentary, *David Kirby on his Deathbed*, was made about the iconic David Kirby photo, joining the ever growing body of work looking back at HIV history. My writing partner, Alexandra Juhasz, and I call this body the "AIDS Crisis Revisitation." Starting after a period of AIDS-related silence emerging after the release of life-saving medication in 1996, the AIDS Crisis Revisitation begins in 2008 with a noticeable increase in the creation, dissemination, and discussion of culture concerned with the early responses to HIV/AIDS. The Revisitation includes but is not limited to the films: *How to Survive a Plague, Dallas Buyers Club;* the exhibitions, *Art AIDS America; One day this kid will grow larger...*, Tim Murphy's novel *Christodora;* Alysia Abbott's memoir *Fairyland;* Tiona McClodden's artwork *Af-fixing Ceremony: Four Movements for Essex, The Uncoolness of Grief;* and the plays *Thirtynothing,* written by Dan Fishback; and *And We Should Stand Like This.* written by Harrison Rivers. Overall, the Revisitation has been positive, carving out space for healing, hearing, and reunion. And yet, as myself and others have noticed, there is a narrowness within the Revisitation. With a few exceptions within the Revisitation, there is an overall absence of people of color, of women, of black people, of trans people, of people in rural America, people who inject drugs, who do sex work, who live in poverty, and people who live at intersections of all of these ways of being alive. I see the work coming out of the AIDS Crisis Revisitation and I think: where are all the people? Why am I only seeing different versions of me? It is not that the story of white gay men in the face of the plague does not matter, it does. It does. It is just that it is not the only story, and in a patriarchal culture of white supremacy, it gets treated as the beginning and the end of the story.

I avoided watching the short film on the David Kirby photo. As someone working at the intersection of art, AIDS and activism, I too up to this moment, as a white, gay, HIV negative middle-class, cis man, have failed to acknowledge Peta and I couldn't bear the thought of the film doing the same. But I was provoked into watching it after attending a panel this summer about queer literature and the panelists discussed both the absence and presence of new AIDS related culture being made. I felt the need to weigh in. So, sitting one night at a writing residency, I watched the film. Early on, Peta appears through photos. I gasped. Would I hear someone other than me and the friend who jump-started my research on the photo say Peta outloud? No. Peta is never named. Referred to only as caregiver. And then, only in passing.

Black feminist ethicist Dr. Traci West tells us that our ethics form where the story begins, and our ethics are revealed in our actions. When you look at the work coming out of the AIDS Crisis Revisitation, the stories often begin—mirroring the focus of the Revisitation—with photos, like the one of David Kirby: a white gay man, to be pitied, to be feared. And so, isn't Dr. West so painfully right? The bulk of our actions in response to HIV have been, and still are, focused on white gay men (or making a big production of it when they are not). So what would it mean if we pulled the camera back, and started the story with that which has been obscured, cut off, neglected? What would it mean if we told the story of HIV though Peta? Through people whose land has been stolen? Through people whose gender the culture refuses to see? What if we told the story of HIV through the visible hand of friendship?

HIV is first and foremost a material reality, which lives in some people's bodies and not in others, the reasons for the disparity, intimate and systemic in scale. It is also a cultural phenomenon, shaped by us. AIDS is a rolling cultural inheritance, a spectacle that looms overhead, shaping prose, poetry and desire. As a fellow writer, I hope you accept this little bit of information I have about Peta, and transmit it to others, replicating the love without fear.

Theodore Kerr is a Brooklyn based writer and organizer whose work focuses primarily on HIV/AIDS. He is a founding member of the collective, What Would an HIV Doula Do? tedkerr.club

Four Moments in a Scene
an excerpt
Danny Thanh Nguyen

One of the rules of our open relationship is that David and I talk about our extracurricular sex lives. This time, our update occurs over dinner.

"So there's this boy," David says. He holds the lit screen of his iPhone across the table. A young man in a blue hoodie with UCLA arched across the front beams at me.

We are at David's favorite Vietnamese hole-in-the-wall restaurant, sitting by a mirror framed by Christmas lights even though it is June. Our waitress has taken our order and is preparing iced coffee in the kitchen. David swipes at his phone, flipping through more photos: a short awkward redhead from a bar, a tanned San Diego tourist.

There is no protocol for how these updates occur; the process just casually happens. We share our hookup stories the way we talk about a news headline we've read.

David is brick-shaped and wears solid black shirts to make himself look slimmer. He is thirty-three years old, but his face is that of a boy's. In order to attract younger men, he advertises himself as twenty-five in his online profiles. The guys he hooks up with are youthful, like little college-aged Chihuahuas in Diesel jeans. Their bodies are smooth and sleek, their faces doe-eyed and curious. As he flashes their photos across his phone, I suddenly feel my own body hair itching beneath my clothes. My beard feels heavier.

When he asks about my latest hookups, I tell him that I haven't had sex recently.

"Really?" he says.

"Really," I say. "Only played."

"Play" is code. For the other stuff. The *not-sex* sex. I haven't abandoned vanilla sex, but lately I've had a trend of meeting guys who like to be tied down and beaten up, or guys who want to do the same to me.

Now David is quiet, tapping his fingers nervously on the glass table. His eyes look glazed. He is fighting to unthink whatever images that have swelled up in his mind. Possibly: me clipping clothespins onto a man's nipples then hitting them off with a riding crop. Possibly: me looking like Pinhead from *Hellraiser* with a leather hood over my head, my mouth panting through the opened zipper-mouth (even though I find these hoods so creepy that they practically auto-safeword themselves from my scenes.)

David shivers inwardly. The waitress delivers our iced coffee to split. And we sit there in so much silence it feels as if a spell has been cast over us.

1.

At this point, I'd like to engage in some role-play. So let's pretend that you are me and I am nowhere and you are ten years old. You are in the living room with your mother, watching television. The couch smells of countless meals she has cooked and you are wearing your favorite Spiderman pajamas. Your mother sits next to you, noting the Closed Captions on the screen because, as an immigrant, this is how she practices her English. Tonight's episode of *Star Trek: The Next Generation* is the one where Captain Jean-Luc Picard is captured by grey-skinned aliens who take him aboard their ship. They strip him naked and cuff his wrists, suspending him off the floor with his arms above his head. His body is exposed: bare legs, chest hair on pale flesh. The aliens torture the Captain by electrocuting him throughout his body. From the way he screams, the tears in his eyes and the ominous swell of the music, you understand that you should be overwhelmed with pity.

You look up at your mother for direction on how to read this vision, but she is busy mouthing the words to the subtitles. You return to the screen, the image of a prisoner being tormented and broken by his captors. You don't understand why you feel conflicted, but the excitement is true: you wish you could be him.

Later that night, when your mother puts you to bed, you ask her to tuck the sheets in extra tight. You like that tight compression holding you down. You are too young, too innocent to understand shame, only desire. You are too young to even comprehend what it means to be sexually aroused, so this desire has no dexterity. It is formless in shape, but it still wraps itself around you. Though you do not realize it yet, you will forever be bound to this yearning.

"What did you do once you had him tied up?" David asks.

We are between bites of our steaming bowls of noodle soup. I can tell the smell of fried garlic will be clinging to my clothes and hair for the rest of the night.

I hesitate to tell David that my last play buddy was deeply into titty torture, that in order to elicit a response I had to twist his nipples so rough that they swelled up like rubber bullets, that I could taste the coppery plasma on my teeth.

I keep my identities separate. For David's sake, I rarely invoke the kinds of play I do unless he asks. If I were to mention ropes and mouth gags, cuffs and whips, he'll wince as if I've pressed on a bruise. He understands that I am wired this way—that it comes naturally and cannot be changed—and the open relationship is one of the ways he shows his support. Still, he finds it intimidating. He tells me that he fears that I will find someone who can give me things he cannot and that I'll be spirited away. I tell him that I like vanilla ice cream as much as I bourbon cornflake with caramel swirls.

When he does ask for details, I keep the answers polite and brief. He is part of that world of normals. Of soft kisses and cheek caresses and cuddles in beds. He sees me as slipping into a world of perverts, a dark wailing place full of roots and torn skin.

After dinner, we slog ourselves down the sidewalk, back to the car to return to our apartment. The savory aroma of soup fills the sedan. When I turn on the ignition, David leans across to kiss me and his lips graze my facial hair.

"Ouch!" he says.

Like my kinks, the hair is also starting to bother him. The night before, we were watching TV on the couch and I stretched my bare legs against his, let the hair on my calves rub across his shin. He pulled away, then pantomimed holding up air-clippers as if he were a barber, and made a buzzing sound. He ran the phantom blades up the length of my leg then he took it to my face—*Bzzzzzz*—like he were shearing a sheep.

I wasn't always an active pervert, nor was I always hairy like I am now. I used to look like those boys whose pictures he collects on his phone. I once had a 29-inch waist and was his ideal twink: smooth, boyish, a little dumb. I was nineteen years old when David and I began dating and now I am nearly thirty. My shoulders have broadened, my metabolism has slowed down, and my belly has begun to slope over my belt.

"Your stubble hurts," David says.

"What hurts," I say, "is having to shave my face everyday to keep it trimmed."

I rest my right hand on David's knee and steer with my left. We drive past closed Laundromats and corner stores with metal bars over their windows. Even though it is nighttime, a man is spraying pigeon shit and litter from the sidewalk in front of his flower shop with a water hose. I stop at a green light for a homeless woman pushing a cart filled with plastic bags across the intersection.

2.

Another urge for role-play. Maybe because I know of no other means of showing you than by way of instruction.

Once again, imagine you are me. This time you are in the living room of a man who you have just met off of Craigslist. He is an attorney (why are these kinksters always lawyers?) who collects foreign antiques and is skilled in Japanese rope bondage, and you are hog-tied facing down on the foam padded floor. Your wrists are restricted behind your back, ankles bent and bound to your thighs, your knees spread eagle. The pressure of the ropes cuts across your chest, arms, stomach, and legs. Your sweat soaks the ropes.

He is aware that your lover is not kinky; that he will be your first bondage scene. He sounded like a normal person on the phone. "Don't worry," he said, "I'm safe and sane." He was even kind enough to ask about your experience level (none), your limits (you're not sure), and even spent half an hour coaching you to the understanding that there will be no fucking, no blood, no piss. This put you at ease.

But now that you're mummified in rope, his body is standing above yours like a threat. He could very well rape you and cut your body into pieces. He could put you into garbage bags and scatter you into the bay. But you trust him only because you want to be able to trust him. You fear the consequences of what could go wrong but your fear, with all its sharp edges, only arouses you further. So you focusing on the warm air flowing in and out of your nose and breathe through the pain of the ropes cutting into the tender part of your armpit. You close your eyes and let blind faith direct you.

I've been telling my friends that my new goal in life is to become a big fat daddy bear. I am half-joking, but I am 100% serious. I believe in striving for obtainable goals.

I repeat the joke to David as we wait for the light to turn green again.

"That's gross," David says.

I tried staving off the natural progression of my weight and body hair through gym routine and an infomercial hair removal product called

Nad's. The latter of which was a green goo on strips of fabric that I stuck to my ass and tugged off to remove the hair—and often skin. I lost plenty of money and blood before accepting that I can't really grow younger and skinnier; I can only grow older and hairier.

One of my favorite Marvel comic book supervillains is The White Queen. She dresses like a drag queen wearing nothing but stark white lingerie, thigh-high boots, a laced-up corset, and mink stole. Her mutant power is telepathy, the ability to influence thought. Over time, she underwent a secondary mutation, like a second puberty. She was still able to read minds, but now she could turn her skin into diamonds for self-defense.

There is another mutant in her world who also underwent a secondary mutation: Hank McCoy, codenamed Beast. His first gift was that of superhuman strength, and then, later in life, he evolved into a big blue furry man-creature.

What I mean to say is: I am a mutant with superpowers. I've undergone several mutations in my lifetime. And despite my kinks making me feel like I'm bedazzled with diamonds, I have begun to look like an unrecognizable hairy beast to my lover.

3.

This time your friend Tim, who you met at a dungeon party, has invited you over for your very first flogging lesson. Because you live in San Francisco, you have access to things like sourdough bread, cable cars, and community dungeons that host S&M parties.

His living room is furnished only with a couch and a flat-screen TV. He hands a flogger to you and shows you how to hold it: fingers wrapped around the hilt.

"Drape the tassels down your back and swing like you're casting a fishing line."

You mimic his motion, noting the weight of the leather tassels.

"Hold the knob at the end of the hilt," he says. You do this.

"Loosen your wrist to control the momentum," he says. You do this also.

He shows you how to swing a figure-8. He makes you practice on the wall, leaving black leather scuffs in the shape of an X on the white paint. After a few rounds, your forearm fatigues. Your wrist aches from the unfamiliar movement.

"Now try it on me," Tim says.

He peels his shirt off, exposing patches of short hairs spread between his shoulders. He turns and presses his hands against the wall. "Aim for the X-shape of my shoulder blades," he says. "Do the figure-8 within the box just below the neck and where my ribcage ends. Got it?"

You find the box and outline it with your eyes. You picture your swing making precise contact. You can't tell if you're over-confident or over-nervous, but you bring the flogger down hard—too hard. The leather wraps around Tim's neck and shoulder and collarbone. A crisp sharp snap cracks his skin. He screams and falls to his knees.

"I'm sorry…" you stammer.

You take a step forward to assess the damage. A long belt of red has already begun to swell by his neck. Dots of popped blood vessels rise to the surface. He takes a moment to come down off the pain. Then picks himself back up.

"Your aim was too high. Remember to start off slow. Warm up the body first."

"Are you okay?" you say.

You lift your hand as if you'd like to offer medical assistance, though you're not exactly sure what you can do. Tim brushes it off.

The refrigerator in the kitchen begins to hum. You hold the flogger loosely in your fingers. You want to drop it. You don't understand the physics of the toy yet, you are afraid of its strength. You tell Tim that you don't want to continue.

"This is going to happen," he says. "You're going to mess up and hurt your partner in the wrong ways by accident. You just need to learn how to get it right."

A play buddy of mine once explained his parents' divorce with an Albert Einstein quote: "Women marry men hoping they will change. Men marry women hoping they will not. So each is inevitably disappointed."

David and I didn't marry women—we married each other. We made appointments to signed legal papers at City Hall. We followed the judge in his robe up to the top of the marble staircase. We recited vows that echoed under the dome.

When the judge asked, "For as long as you both shall live?" we both said our I Do's. We slipped white gold bands onto each other's fingers, understanding the gravity that we would forever be bound to each other. We had that much faith.

I wonder how successful married couples do it: grow old and happy together, especially when one or both are bound to turn into different people over time. I can't decide who David saw when he looked into my eyes at the top of that staircase, impossibly handsome in his black suit as he said that he would love and care for me. Did he think he was marrying a man who happened to be a kinkster that had changed into someone he found acceptable? Or maybe he saw a kinkster who would eventually change into someone who he would found acceptable? Or maybe he thought he married a kinkster who would not change, but he could learn to accept. One of these is true. None of these is true. Or perhaps: all of these are true.

There are bridges that you cross as you grow older, each of them leading to destinations different from where you started. You don't always choose these bridges nor do you choose where they lead you. Becoming a kinky daddy bear is a realistic bridge, something intuitive and realistic. When I will have crossed onto the other side of that bridge, I wonder if David will still be attracted by what he sees. Or will he be back on the other side, repeating his I Do's to a ghost of me.

4.

David is my lover and he does not know how to do anything but make love to me. He has no sense of roughness, no inner demon to inspire sadism. The last time we made love, it was a night that was too hot for San Francisco, where the muggy air in the apartment stalled in its place like a wool blanket. We were irritated from the weather and each other, had been fighting and fighting and eventually somehow found the resolution, like we always do, after hours of yelling. We had finished having makeup sex—the act of trying to push ourselves back together until we were a single cohesive being again—and were lying in a pool of sweat and cum and all the nameless magical elements that exists which bonds two people together before they go spiraling away from each other again.

I got up to go to the bathroom. When I came back, David was fast asleep, snoring. He was splayed out across the bed we shared, with an arm reaching over the side, as if he's trying to reach out and tug me towards him with his fingers. At least that's what I told myself. It's an image I needed to see when looked down at the space he made available in order to find my place.

Danny Thanh Nguyen is the editor of AS IS, an anthology of Vietnamese American literature, and is a Kundiman Fellow. His fiction and personal essays have appeared in The Journal, South Dakota Review, Gulf Coast, New Delta Review, Entropy, and more.

Fascinum
Rajat Singh

A boy on the subway touched me. Not in the way a body falls into yours, as the train sways and suddenly lurches, matter speeding through tenebrous tunnels. Not in the way your body presses back, unthinkingly, as if to support a stranger, help him catch himself, reassure him he's not alone in his liability. No, this boy, he sat in his seat, facing me, and found himself searching.

Every minute or so, he raised his head toward me, then titled his face tilted downward, tucked his chin into his chest. He bored into me, then looked away to tap at the phone lit in his lap, to fumble with the tangled cord he was inserting into its base. He lifted his eyes toward me, then averted them to linger on another face.

The F train was barreling into Manhattan, on my way home from the therapist's office. Underground tunnels, running through the river that separates the boroughs, transform the glass of the subway window into a black mirror. I'm used to seeing myself reflected, but not this time. Narcissus' view was blocked, unable to slip into the pool of his own appearance.

I saw the boy's face roving and so it was that I went here and there rather than stay with him on his search. My eyes didn't follow the angle of my neck but instead traced other faces, more attractive ones, those they preferred to remain gazing on. My sunglasses made me confident in my sneakiness. Yet my eyes returned to him. He kept inviting me into the ocean that was drowning him.

Everyone who endures New York City public transportation learns how to navigate the system's rules for making and avoiding eye contact. I've made a diversion out of catching other people's stares. Sometimes they look at me and I apprehend them with the flick of my eyes. They me make me feel known, even wanted. There's also a sort of second-order observation I practice: catching people staring at others. Picture the woman I once saw curling her eyelashes with a spoon on her morning commute. As I prayed for the train not to stop abruptly and land her in the E.R., I noticed a man glaring at her over his newspaper, his face registering a curious mixture of fascination and revulsion. I've long triangulated encounters like this, observing, assured and safe, from the sidelines. I make a sport out of it, free myself the ethics of getting involved. Looking fills me with a voyeuristic thrill, as if I'm not implicated in the attention strangers cast on strangers. 9/11 gave us the mass-transit directive, "If you see something, say something," but I prefer to consider what makes a glance unwanted and what makes it welcome. Who gets to look?

Roland Barthes calls cruising "drifting" or "skidding." Trains cannot veer off their tracks without risking serious casualties or even a crash. But bodies are more flexible—and perhaps the better for it—they get to be vulnerable, and reach out when they're in need. Veering into another's lane is this sexual readiness. It's a language like many others, in that it's taught, but it's also an orientation, a stance, "a willingness to pick up codes," as Barthes writes.

One bright fall afternoon, a decade earlier, a brown-skinned man read my longing. As I scanned the car, swaying to the Hindi music slipping through my earbuds, he looked at me from the end of the car and didn't look away until he moved closer to me, to a seat directly in front of me, pinning me to my defenselessness. I don't know how I knew he wanted me, other than the fact that his actions terrified me at the same time that they excited me. His behavior defied the norms of conventional looking. I was riding home to see my parents—an engagement I, for longer than a second, considered ditching for a man who held me fast in an empty train car. If he wanted me, he didn't use his words to tell me. His desire was couched in coded language: a steady, piercing gaze, legs spread toward me.

I smiled at him, stopping just short of fully acknowledging him or letting him know I was interested. All he was looking for, all he needed, was a moment. He pushed on, as if he'd been invited, drawing his hand to the outline in his lap. He offered himself to me, and I grew more nervous the deeper he bored inside, into a place unmapped on any anatomical chart. Still, I didn't want to be released.

In Latin, a *fascinum* was both a magic spell as well as a phallic charm worn around a child's neck to ward off the evil eye. Casting a look that rendered one unable to move or resist was the power of *invidia,* from the Latin meaning "looking on." The eye enchants, renders another powerless.

To my surprise—both shock and secret thrill—the man reached across his lap to his hip pocket and pulled out of his jeans a stack of folded twenties. The tension broke instantly, the charge blown. I could have used the money but in that instant, I realized I'd have to keep my date with my parents. My face twisting in fear, I fumbled for the cord to request a stop—one too soon.

I hadn't brought my sunglasses—it was bright, but I'd forgotten them in my dorm room. And I couldn't close my eyelids. Still, I needed a way to say without words that this wasn't the game I wanted to play, or the way I wanted to be wanted. I stepped off the train, disgusted at myself— and not at someone who was making up new rules.

On the historical significance of cruising, J. Bryan Lowder writes, "gayness begins in the practice of paying attention, deeply and with great skill." This heightened attunement both protects and connects gay men within dominant, heteronormative settings. Cruising, Lowder notes, demands an almost obsessive awareness to nuance. Gayness way back when was in the details—the angle of a wrist, say, or an irreverent flower tucked into a lapel. Zeroing in on subtlety could convey volumes of information—whether you were in good company, about to get laid, or casting a fruitless gaze. Perhaps one can even say looking saves lives. Learning how to look isn't simply an act of seeing the present, but readying oneself for the future. It anticipates the possibility for community as it demonstrates openness.

To return to the boy on the subway, not the man, but the boy, who continued to shift in his seat and make me uneasy. His gaze was a vernacular altogether foreign to me and I struggled to read what he was saying. Without any information, I erased him and replaced him with myself. I went so far as to think the boy could've been me.

He was of South Asian origin, his skin a shade or two browner than mine. Youthful, pensive, and full of disquiet. He had closely cropped black hair. His jawline cut a sharp angle. A tight, black leather perfecto and black fitted jeans matched my own sartorial style. He sat completely closed off to the world. Thin knees bowed toward one another—lest he take up too much space on the long bench. Shoulders hunched inward— maybe to protect a heart recently battered. His neck bent forward—as if the world's weight were too heavy to withstand. His body contorted into itself but I thought it was calling out to me, shuddering. His lips either mouthed the lyrics of whatever was warbling through his headphones. Or they parted, chanting prayers to fortify himself against the dangers of the world. My headphones in and my sunglasses on, I rode along inaccessible. Still, it was his eyes that pierced me—their restlessness making me worry about him and me, maybe more me than him. He seemed too weak to live his questions. I imagined I was looking at a me I'd buried deep within myself.

The boy fixated on the subway passengers and his eyes dulled with weary indignation. Neither the Latino kids cutting school, nor the gaggle of white gay guys gossiping down at the other side of the car— none of them were available to him. His were hollow eyes, roving beyond the invisible boundaries we'd all constructed and consented to in the train car. He shook his head from side to side, slowly, musically. I sensed he was pleading for someone to tune in. He reached out, but not like the man who had read and transacted my own longing years ago, who'd made me ashamed that I wanted what he was offering. Rather, I assumed I could read this boy's aching. Yet I felt more ashamed than if I'd taken the cash.

Empathy risks appropriating another's suffering, of making it one's own. I say to myself, he could've been me were circumstances different. But what does this identification get me? Is it selfish to echo his aching with my deafening unavailability? Or more selfish, invisibly so, to see myself in his ostensible pain?

Just like that, my stop came and I stood up. I hurried off the car, too scared to look back. I was immediately calmed by my own ability to flee. This time, and the time a decade earlier, I'd been transfixed, rendered paralyzed, as if by a spell. Each encounter was decidedly different, but both times I'd struggled to sift my desire from disgust from the powerlessness I experienced in the face of that which confounded me most: not another person, but myself. Getting another's attention can have so many meanings. I thought it was up to me to learn the semiotics of a look.

Rajat Singh is working on a collection of essays examining queer melancholy through South Asian culture.

Butterfly People
(originally published in BOAAT Journal)
Steffan Triplett

"In time of silver rain
the earth puts forth new life again,"
-Langston Hughes

In grade school we grew monarchs in plastic bins. We sat in rows, learning times tables in exchange for ice cream toppings. Each day was simple, each day was boring, until the last. Metamorphosis: a change in nature of a life into something wholly different. A worm, to a pod, to wonder. One day we walked into the classroom and saw orange wings where none had been before. *These butterflies always return home*, we were taught. Not a full-truth, but we smiled at the promise of predictable life.

We went outside to give the butterflies a life more natural—*a mother must let go of her kids*, we were told, a lesson within a lesson. Our teacher removed a green topper, but the beings clung to their walls. She gave the bin a shake. They fluttered onto the grass and enjoyed a moment of bliss in the breeze.

Suddenly, a boy stomped on them. He laughed. The sun was shining. I wiped tears from my eyes, upset the butterflies never had the chance to fly. We buried the crumpled beauties in dirt, covered them in dried grass. A promise extinguished in front of us.

*

I think of *butterfly people* and my mind funnels. I picture humans not with arms, but symmetric wings, brown shattered-glass lines and matching ovals on each side. These beings smile and look at themselves with wet eyes of wonder—they shouldn't exist. I wonder if butterfly wings are strong enough to hold the weight of human life. Can they fly without help from the wind?

A mural in old downtown commemorates the day the creatures swirled in. On the corner of 15th and Main, on the exposed wall of the Dixie Printing building, there are paintings of butterflies, or people, or children, or aliens—antennae and all. I've never seen them before, only viewed their images here, only heard about them in whispers.

The mural wears a partial Hughes poem:

"In time of silver rain
the butterflies lift silken wings
to catch a rainbow cry,
and trees put forth
new leaves to sing
in joy beneath the sky."

I don't like to imagine the trees singing. Not our trees—trees without limbs are a sad song, a somber melody in minor key. I can still hear it when I look at them. Now, they stand dismembered and twisted. Some saw a rainbow that day. A rainbow and butterflies. I thought God was done flooding Earth long ago.

*

In fourth grade we learned that Langston Hughes was from Joplin. He wasn't here long—*the place you were born doesn't always stay home.* Our lessons grew heavier with age. The teacher asked me to perform a poem in front of the class. Dream Variations. I added motions to his words.

"Dance, Whirl, Whirl," I sung.

I spun around and around, smiling in both joy and embarrassment. I pointed to my skin at the poem's end:

"Night coming tenderly,
Black like me."
Kids laughed at my spinning. Dizzied, I returned to my seat.

The poem felt different now. It wasn't the same as when I practiced in the living room at home. I felt my presence and body in the spins in front of classmates I didn't look like. It was the first time I wanted to flee.

Was he really from here of all places? Was he loved? We learned that Langston died far away from home, on the twenty-second day of May. Did he ever dream of coming back? I wonder if the sun shone at his funeral.

*

That day the sky changed. That day another promise was broken. That day the sky turned majestic and mean. It was all types of color. The rain went sideways.

For 38 minutes, a storm came through home, the sky an odd gray. A Sunday. A storm came through Joplin and left all these broken trees, and homes, and bodies. It left all these dreams. People let go of their kids. Their parents. Their love. On the twenty-second day of May, we handed over gifts to the gray arm of the sky.

Children in town saw butterfly people. They saw them with their eyes, in their minds, in their dreams. The story is common now. Folklore like that dizzy day. Spinning wind. Twirling rains. People launched into the air.

"Wasn't it pretty? They were carrying people into the sky," a child tells her mother.

It's how the kids explain what happened. It's how they were protected. It's how they know their lost loved ones are safe now. *Did you see the butterfly people?* Wasn't it pretty? These butterflies always return home.

I'm not sure I believe in angels. I don't want to know how it feels to fly.

*

I wonder what's real. Bodies swirling in a gray mass of wind. Limbs removed. Heads upturned. Humans shaped wrong. I try not to imagine, but I see them in my dreams. 162 dead butterflies. 162 crumpled bodies. 162 people dead because of wind. We prayed the damage was done but were still finding bodies days later.

Tornado—I spiral when I hear the word. I fear the air when I hear it wail. I fear the sky when it turns purple or green or silver. I don't like to return to my changed home in spring. We're not in Missouri anymore. We're somewhere else.

"Green grasses grow
and flowers lift their heads
And over all the plain
the wonder spreads."

Hughes dedicated his poem to a dying friend. Did he believe his own words? At home I think of butterfly people and I dream of flying away.

Steffan Triplett is an MFA candidate and instructor at the University of Pittsburgh. Some of his work appears or is forthcoming in DIAGRAM, The Offing, BOAAT, Underblong, The Shade Journal, Essay Daily, Red Paint Hill, Kweli Journal, and Nepantla: An Anthology for Queer Poets of Color, and WILDNESS where it was nominated for Best of the Net. Steffan is an alum of VONA and the Callaloo Creative Writing Workshop. He was raised in Joplin, Missouri.

Constant Erasure
originally published in Different Skies
Ricky Tucker

The mountainside campground was plucked out of an act from Briga-doon–except nobody was Scottish. Actually, somebody might have been Scottish, but the majority of us weren't. Rewind. The bride was a childhood friend/perpetual orchestra stand partner, and everyone in her party was someone I'd known since forever. The groom and his entire half of the wedding party were Irish. We'd all flown in from various parts of the globe forming what I imagine on a map looks like a large and leafy palm tree. A shorter branch would be my brief flight from Boston, and the long and enduring trunk would be that of the Australian whom I'd later follow, hand in hand, into the woods during a particularly tricky patch of square dance instructions.

The X-mark was Camp Pinnacle, a sleep-away camp east of the Smoky Mountains in North Carolina. It was far enough (a few hours' drive) from our Winston-Salem, NC homes, and with the Irish brogues bouncing all around the place, it felt like a destination.

We stayed together in bunks, some of us for the second or third time in our lives, and later, in the cool blue a.m., we'd sneak back into the mess hall for second helpings of barbequed brisket, chopped slaw, and corn pudding. We hummed with the mischief of whichever Irish beer we'd tried too much of for the first time. We were kids again but adults.

I brushed the pine needles from my hands and knees and walked into the light of the now swinging barn. The Australian followed me five beats behind. My oldest and number one ace, 'Z', was bored with clapping for her fiancé who was dosey-doeing merrily but slowly with somebody's great aunt. Instead, 'Z' focused her attention on me, the Australian, and our ill-paced procession. I sat next to her and tried not to smirk.

"Where did you just come from," she said squinting.

"The woods over there…"

"Oh my god. You're such a whore."

"Ha! Whatever."

We laughed for a second as her fiancé dipped Gertrude to the floor and back up again.

"How did that happen?"

"I dunno," I said. "We were talking and the next thing I knew, he was leading me into the bush, so to speak."

She looked off into the distance, half smiling and shaking her head as if baffled.

"You're so mysterious."

I didn't know what to say. The fact that she'd known me since I was nine years old and still considered me mysterious felt like an accomplishment of sorts. Without meaning to be, I was a puzzle she couldn't quite work out. Ricky Tucker: eluding the comprehension of loved ones for over twenty years. I'll take it, I thought, until she said, "You know he only did it because you're black."

Again, I didn't know what to say.

Had I responded, I would have asked her how exactly she found it possible for anyone to bypass my smile, winning personality, and general attractiveness to arrive at such a basic point. I also would have said so what. We're all a composite of stats that form our sexual experience; why pluck race out of that pile? I could have gone into a diatribe about the etymology of words like 'mysterious' and how they run rampant in texts like *Heart of Darkness*. I wanted to start a genuine conversation with her about how as a species humans give priority to sight – how this one sense out of five can still revert, at moments like these, to associations more Cro-Magnon than fully Homo sapiens. Finally, I would have told her that she shouldn't go around just saying everything she thought. It's simple and rude. But I didn't say anything. Instead, I continued clapping, watching aunt Dorothy delight in being twirled around – weightless and young again.

* * *

A black man walks into a bar.
He looks up and says, "Who said that?"

* * *

When under duress, I have a go-to mantra: I wish to fly.

I suppose it's more of a wish than a mantra because of the word 'wish', but functions more like a mantra in my repetition of it. I wish to fly, I wish to fly, I wish to fly – until the rough patch passes. It may actually be a nervous tick.

I will say, as a straightforward wish, its effectiveness has yet to be seen; I am very much tethered to this earth. Still, I don't think it wise for one to judge the merit of a wish based on how quickly or literally said wish is granted. The point of a wish is hope, and once it's granted, the thing lies dead like a shell.

For me, a wish's true brilliance is in the construction of the wish itself. What is your central desire, and how well can you package and deliver it, ensuring all of its air holes are sealed shut?

* * *

Genies are notoriously sketchy motherfuckers. This is why, in my preteens, I changed the wording of my wish/mantra from "I wish I *could* fly" to "I wish to fly." It's all in the copy.

Imagine spending the greater part of a decade trudging through sand dunes and caves to find Aladdin's lamp. Finally, you find it. You rub it. From the lamp's mouth, a glorious genie extends in all his blue smoke and mind-blowing opulence. You almost freak, but instead you gather your moxie; this is your moment after all. He speaks to you.

"Oh, noble and gracious son of man. You have freed me from centuries of imprisonment. What wish might I grant you in exchange for this deed?"

"Hmmm. A wish…" you say, rubbing your chin. "I haven't thought too much about it. Well, there is one thing I've always wanted…"

"Mm-hm," says the genie. He's seen centuries of false modesty and is unimpressed by yours.

"I got it," you say unconvincingly. "I wish I could fly!"

"As you wish," he says, floating up to his full height.

You plop down in a half squat with both fists clenched in front of you, your eyes reduced to slits, waiting for the magic to happen.

Nothing happens. You get your tall-tales mixed for a moment and start thinking happy thoughts to move the process along, but nope, you're still grounded. Continuing to brace yourself, your left eye wrenches open to find the genie, standing with one hand on his hip and the other covering his mouth. He seems to be dying of silent laughter.

"Hey, what gives?" you scream. "I said, 'I wish I could fly!'"

"And you *could* fly," says the Genie, "If you were a bird, silly goose."

* * *

A black man, Asian man, and Muslim man walk into a bar. The black man takes note of the narrator's formal inconsistency and says, "Oh, I get it. This is some kind of joke."

* * *

A man walks into a bar. Even before arriving, he knows the Boston establishment to be unsavory in that it caters to fraternity types–less commonly dreaded but just as riff-raff an element as any. "Oh, well," he says to himself, "wings and beer are the great equalizers." He removes his gloves and sits, waiting for his academic brothers to show.

Half a pint later, he welcomes his two tweed-jacketed friends to the table. They are lively and in good spirits as the afternoon sun has wrestled the New England frost to the ground.

One friend starts with a, "Hey, hey!" The other gentleman, while pulling out a wooden stool, smiling, and uncoiling his satin scarf from his neck, says, "I hope this place is okay. I had my concerns."

Thinking it prudent for now to reserve his own fleeting prejudices regarding the bar's clientele, the first man says, "What concerns were those?"

"Well, I thought to myself," his friend begins, "I wonder if I made a mistake picking this place. I wouldn't want Ricky to be the only black person in the room."

"It's fine," I say.

* * *

Color blindness. Here's the thing: I've never been oblivious to race and neither have you. It's damn near impossible, and when you say you are it smacks of tragic cliché like when people assure you they could never be too skinny or rich, or are certain that all animals go to heaven. Enough.

What's more interesting, but just as impossible, is the concept of being blind to one's *own* race. Again, it can't be done. But as a person of color, and general observer of the world, I can tell you that there are times when you are completely whole and content within, focused mostly on spaces outside of yourself, and you slip up and become, if only partially or momentarily, less aware of your own physical assignment on earth. You don't see yourself, and every bit of what you see before you, people, relationships, grass, is meant to be there. Everything full of grace. And that perfectly selfless moment of Zen is precisely when one of your white friends, without provocation, comes right along to remind you that you are certifiably, inescapably, and unfortunately black.

* * *

A man grows a third eye that allows him to see into the fourth dimension. When exposed, the eye receives from the astral plane transcripts of people's shittiest thoughts and delivers them to the man's brain. He finds this a bother and takes to wearing a black blindfold over the extra eye. His friends in turn take to calling him 'Kung-Fu Larry'. Instead of shaking his hand, they chop the air in front of him, saying "Hi-yah!" instead of "Hello." When he walks by a dojo everyone bows, and his girlfriend buys him a full-on black belt ensemble because, "Mama likey this new look."

He removes the blindfold and says "Sayonara!" as he jumps from the town bridge.

* * *

A black man walks into a bar and immediately exits through the kitchen.

Ricky Tucker is a North Carolina native, storyteller, essayist, and art critic. His work often explores the imprint of art on narrative, and the absurdity of most fleeting moments. He received his BA in fiction from The New School in NYC, and a Writer/Teacher MA at Goldsmiths, University of London.

PLAYWRITING

Started From The Convent Now We're Here
an excerpt
s.a.b.u.

A cathedral. There are strobe lights, fog machines raging, and house music pumping. There are nuns and monks grooving. They are in varying stages of undress with some crossdressing mixed in for good measure. Asses out. Tits out. Dicks out. A couple vaginas out because why not? There are glow sticks and perhaps a burst of glitter. Actually, *fuck yea* - bursts of glitter. Two nuns, AGATHA and MARY are dancing together somewhere around center stage.

AGATHA
Great party, right?

MARY
It's fine.

AGATHA
Bullshit. This party is bananas.

AGATHA gestures to a semi-disrobed monk aggressively riding one of the Jesuses on a crucifix suspended in the air to the beat of the music. Yes, there are a couple of those and a massive disco ball.

MARY
Whatever. I need to take a leak.

AGATHA
Use one of the confessional booths over there.

MARY
Yea?

AGATHA
I mean unless you want to wait in line forever.

The hanging Jesuses make up our Chorus.

CHORUS
Ain't nobody got time for that.

MARY
Ain't nobody got time for that.

CHORUS
True.

AGATHA
That's my girl.

MARY
Alright be right back.

MARY grooves off to one side of the confessional both. AGATHA gets low and PAUL, a monk crossdressed as a nun, comes up behind her. As MARY opens the confessional booth the door breaks off and a monk covered in puke falls out taking a chamberpot down with him, splashing piss, shit, and puke, on the stage.

MARY
Whatever.

MARY opens the other side of the confessional booth and gets to business. The music changes.

AGATHA
Don't you just love this song?

PAUL
Oh my god, yes.

AGATHA
Yes!

PAUL
Yes!

AGATHA
Yea!

CHORUS
Woop Woop!

AGATHA
Damn!

PAUL
Hell yea!

They keep grooving. BERNIE who has been dancing on a block, jumps down and grooves over to them.

BERNIE
Got room for one more?

PAUL
Get in!

PAUL makes space and BERNIE becomes PB&J to their sandwich. MARY exits her confessional booth. She grooves over to the group getting behind AGATHA.

MARY
Hey!

BERNIE
Sup?

PAUL
Sup?

AGATHA
Welcome back!

MARY
Thanks. What a relief.

AGATHA
What?

MARY
What a relief.

AGATHA
Yea. That's good.

MARY
Yea.

AGATHA
Right.

MARY
So who are these guys?

AGATHA
I dunno. You left me and they came over.

MARY
Oh. Okay.

AGATHA
They're good dancers.

MARY
Yea. They're alright. What do they want?

AGATHA
What do they want?

MARY
Yea. What do they want?

BERNIE
to AGATHA
What's your friends name?

AGATHA
Mary. What's your name?

BERNIE
Bernie. What's your name?

AGATHA
Agatha. What's his name?

BERNIE
Fuck if I know.
to PAUL
what's your name?

PAUL
It's Paul.

BERNIE
Nice.

PAUL
Yea. I like it.

MARY
pulling AGATHA to the side
I'm over this. Can we go home?

AGATHA
You wanna go home? We've been looking forward to this all week. I mean, we paid cover.

CHORUS
Ewww. Cover.

MARY
Yea, I know. I just don't know if I'm up to it anymore.

AGATHA
Is it the dudes?

MARY
No, I mean they're fine.

AGATHA
I just figured I was doing us a solid in setting us up for the orgy later... I mean you did say you were hoping for nothing less than two screaming orgasms.

MARY
Yea I know, I know.

AGATHA
Then what is it?

MARY
It's just. I'm just in my head, I guess. I feel like I'm forgetting something.

AGATHA
I mean, Mary. Look around you.

One of the riders of the Jesuses erupts in screams of pleasure and fireworks go off inside the building. The rest of the crowd cheers as the dance party begins transitioning into an orgy.

MARY
I know. I know. I don't know what's wrong with me.

AGATHA
Are you sure?

MARY

No, I'm lying.

AGATHA

You suck. I hate sarcasm.

MARY

I just want to be free.

AGATHA

Free from what?

MARY

Free from thought.

AGATHA

Yea?

MARY

I feel like I started from convent and now I'm here, but I don't know where to go next.

AGATHA

Dude, just fucking live your life.

MARY

I know right. But what is life anyway?

AGATHA

Dude, cut the shit.

MARY

Why? Why, Agatha?

AGATHA

Because you're killing the mood.

MARY

Am I, Agatha?

AGATHA

Yes. Yes you are. We didn't come out to New Jersey's hottest ecclesiastical sex party to ponder life and shit. We came here to dance our asses off, fuck our brains out, and ride a swinging Jesus or two.

MARY

That *was* the dream, wasn't it?

AGATHA

Was? It *is* the dream. Like you said, started from the convent now we're here. Let's do this damn thing.

s.a.b.u. is a genderqueer, mixed race, first generation American playwright, poet, actor, and performance artist. Themes explored have included sex, addiction, race, gender issues, sexual identity, feminism, reproductive rights, ageism, classism, and abuse. (@igetintothings)

House of Franzia
a tasteless play in a recognizable box
Maxe Crandall

Scene 1

The lights slowly rise. At first there are only noises. Grunts and inhalations, the sniffing of animals. Soon those noises turn to chants, and those chants turn to howls, and those howls turn back into chants.

Then, there they are: the men of Pi Kappa Alpha. The Pikes.

PIKES (CHORUS)

RAH RAH FUCK

RAH RAH FUCK

We're PI KAPPA ALPHA
We're RIDERS OF THE NIGHT
We're DIRTY SONS OF BITCHES
Who'd RATHER FUCK THAN FIGHT

Tighty Whitey Christ Almighty
Who the hell are WE?
God damn, old man
We're GREEK FRATERNITY

SHIT PISS SON OF A BITCH
rah rah fuck &
FLIP THAT SWITCH

RAH RAH FUCK
FUCK FUCK RAH
RAH RAH LIKES
RAH RAH PIKES
We're PI KAPPA ALPHA
THE ALPHAS on BIKES

The PIKES cheer. From the middle of the huddle a figure emerges.

MIKE PIKE

Yeah!
  Yeah, I rushed Pikes last year.
It was hella awesome.

  (over his shoulder to his brothers,)
PI KAPPA ALPHA ALL NIGHT LONG!

  (back to the audience,)
Yeah,
  seriously
I never imagined I'd get into my dream school
And then I never thought I'd get into my dream fraternity.
I mean,
  Fuck!

Maybe next year I'll get my dream internship!
I guess that's why they call it a dream job,
huh, when you get your dream job?

Because that job was always something you
vaguely dreamed about doing and then
suddenly fuck: it's happening to you.

Just like all of this hella awesome shit has happened to me.
In college!

PIKES (CHORUS)

FUCK YEAH RAH FUCK RAH RAH

MIKE PIKE

Yeah!
And tonight is my first
Tour de Franzia!

PIKES (CHORUS)

FUCK YEAH RAH RAH

MIKE PIKE

A Tour de Franzia is like this Greek thing
where you fucking flip out with your brothers
and get hella wrecked.

PIKES (CHORUS)

YEAH FUCK RAH

MIKE PIKE

Yeah!
Tonight I'm gonna take boxed wine
out of the box and fucking funnel that sunset shit
down my fucking boat throat and ride my bike
like Lance Fucking Armstrong
all over Franzia!

PIKES (CHORUS)

FUCK YEAH RAH RAH

MIKE PIKE

Yeah!

And I'm gonna do it over and over again
until I'm the fucking winner! The winner of the
Tour de Franzia!

PIKES (CHORUS)

RAH YEAH RAH YEAH

MIKE PIKE

Yeah!

When I fucking win the fucking Tour de Franzia,
I'm gonna pick up some girl next to me. I don't even
care who because California girls are the hottest
and Pikes get the best girls and I'm gonna kiss her!
I'm just gonna lay a long French one on her face
And I bet I'm gonna hold a trophy in the other hand
And I'm gonna be so wrecked
And so happy

It's gonna be a dream night.

PIKES (CHORUS)

RAH RAH RIGHT

MIKE PIKE

Another dream night at Pi Kappa Alpha.

Am I right, brothers?

PIKES (CHORUS)

FUCK YEAH MIKE

FUCK YEAH PIKES

    (one brother hands him a bag of red Franzia.)

MIKE PIKE

    (slapping the bag,)

ARM - STRONG!

PIKES (CHORUS)

RAH RAH RAH RAH

MIKE PIKE

    (slapping the bag,)

DRINK - STRONG!

PIKES (CHORUS)

    (circling around MIKE,)

FUCK FUCK FUCK FUCK

RAH RAH RAH RAH

MIKE PIKE

Fuck! Fuck! Shit! Piss!

    MIKE screams.

PIKES CHORUS

RAH RAH. . . WHAT?

Scene 2

A posh tasting room at one of Napa Valley's finest vineyards. MAN and
WOMAN, wearing the golden masks of gods, sit at a table for two. MAN
pours them each a glass of white wine. They taste it in sync and consider.

WOMAN
    (after some time,)
This is terrible wine.

MAN
Not fit to drink.

    A long pause.

MAN
It's piss.

WOMAN
Frankly is.

Another long pause.

MAN
Do you know what the ancient Greeks did with bad wine?

WOMAN
Why don't you open a bottle from our reserve, and you can tell me all
about it?

*Maxe Crandall loves the Lambda playwrights <3 His book, The Nancy Reagan
Collection, is forthcoming from Futurepoem.*

The Canyon
Freddy Edelhart

This is an interactive piece of theatre!

Don't worry! You don't have to interact if you don't want to.

I am going to ask a question. If your answer to that question is "Yes", raise your hand! Then we'll repeat that process. I will be answering these questions along with you.

You can lie. You can raise your hand every time or not at all. You can leave. You can cover your eyes. I have no control over what you do in response to my questions. But I think it'll be more fun if you answer them.

Okay! Are you ready? Let's get started.

Who here has had sex?

Who here has had good sex?

Who here has had bad sex?

Who here is single?

Who here is romantically partnered in some way?

Who here has been romantically partnered in some way?

Who here has had sex with someone whose name they didn't know?

Who here has had sex with someone whose name they have since actively tried to forget?

Who here hasn't had sex in the past few hours?

Who here hasn't had sex in the past few days?

Who here wants to have sex with someone else at the retreat? ;) ;) ;)

Who here already HAS??? ;) ;) ;) ;)

Who here hasn't had sex in the past few weeks?

Who here hasn't had sex in the past year?

Who here hasn't had sex in the past few years?

Who here has felt loneliness?

Who here has felt loneliness in a physically painful way?

Who here has felt loneliness so physically painful it made it difficult or impossible for them to do other things?

Who here has wondered if their loneliness would ever end?

Who here is still wondering if their loneliness will ever end?

Who here has told themselves, "You know what, it's fine. I don't need sex to be happy. I don't need that kind of companionship to be happy." ?

Who here has realized the above statement is a lie, at least for them?

Who here has had to find new ways to be happy even though the above statement is a lie?

Who here is proud of themselves for finding new ways to happy, but would still much rather be in a relationship than keep being this lonely?

Who here is monogamous?

Who here is polyamorous?

Who here is unsure if they can call themselves polyamorous until they can find like one person to date again?

Who here is bitter?

Who here is bitter in ways that surprise them?

Who here has pretended to be okay for so long they eventually just became okay again?

Who here has gone through this cycle more than once?

Who here has no idea if they will ever break free of that cycle?

Who here has expressed interest in someone, and had that interest reciprocated, but then the person you express interest in changes their mind within a few hours or encounters?

Who here has only had this happen to them over the past few years?

Who here has confided in a dear friend about the above many times?

Who here has had that dear friend propose the two of you have sex a little while later?

Who here has been in love with a dear friend?

Who here has been overjoyed because there is a chance someone they are in love with might love them back?

Who here loves or has loved being partnered because you love your partner, but also because having a partner means neither of you are single and that's good?

Who here loves or has loved being partnered because you love your partner, but also because having a partner means you will probably have more sex than you would if you were single?

Who here loves or has loved being partnered because you love your partner, but also because having a partner means, if someone asks you about your love life, you will have someone to talk about?

Who here has thought they would have someone to talk about and been mistaken?

Who here has thought a situation they were in couldn't possibly get any worse, and then it does?

Who here has fallen into their love for a dear friend they've confided in many times, kissed that friend, and then had that friend change their mind within a few hours?

Who here is still wondering if that friend is ever going to talk to them again?

Who here is still wondering why they want that friend to talk to them again?

Who here has blamed themselves for unexpectedly feeling physically painful amounts of loneliness?

Who here loves people they don't always like or trust?

Who here loves themselves even though they don't always like or trust themselves?

Who here has wondered if there's something wrong with them?

Who here has been taught that their loneliness is extremely unsexy?

Who here is pretty sure that, by performing this piece, they are basically obliterating their chances of getting laid at this retreat?

Who here is pretty sure that, if they're being honest with themselves, they probably weren't going to get laid anyway?

Who here is still hoping, despite everything, that someone will prove them wrong?

Who here is still hoping, despite everything, that they will prove themselves wrong?

Who here is terrified more often then they would like to admit?

Who here has gone on a walk alone at night?

Who here has stood in the middle of the fountain in Washington Square Park in the middle of the night when it's cold and dry?

Who here has stood in the middle of the fountain in Washington Square Park in the middle of the night when it's cold and dry, held their arms up to the sky, and said

I am just an interactive piece of theatre. But don't worry. You don't have to interact if you don't want to.

but

if you do

and if you're looking for me

I am right here?

I am right here.

I am right here.

I am right here.

I am right here...

Keep saying it until you believe it. Once you believe it, the piece ends.

Freddy Edelhart is a devised theatremaker who uses game design to tell stories. Learn more about them and their work at freddyedelhart.com. <3!

The O Word
a monologue
Daniel K. Isaac

I'm not racist

I just don't date OriAsian guys

Don't

Don't make it about

Don't make it about the fact that I'm a cisgender white male who almost

said the O word

I minored in gender studies

I know what cis means

And I know I almost said

Oriental

There

That word

Oh no I said it

And it's not like it's as bad as the other word

That begins with an N

I'm not even gonna say that word

Even though it makes my point stronger

I won't say it

And repeat trauma

Or echo the oppression

The O word does not carry the same weight as the N word

It doesn't have the same history

It's not as bad

It's not

You can't tell me it is

I minored in Ethnic Studies

Oriental

I just got back from living in London and that's what they called East
Asians
Oriental is for people from India in the UK
So
The word doesn't even carry the same
Same
Youknow
And
You're not a rug
You're not an exoticized thing
Or peoples
I'm not reducing you to a color
A shade
I burn in the sun
You tan
I'd kill to at least freckle
Freckle under almond shaped brown eyes
Do you know how boring it is to have blue eyes
Oh no they match with everything blue
And turn green when I wear green
And grey when I wear grey
Bo-ring
The straight black hair
I'd kill to have your hair
Do you know how much sea salt spray I have to use on this
The amount of blow drying
And the three other types of hair spray that maintains this volume
Without getting flaky
To achieve effortless bed head appeal
Framing your flat face
No I like my profile
I recently renovated my bathroom with one of those tri-folding mirrors
and it's Great for getting the cowlicks out of the back of your head after an

afternoon nap
But I also like
Didn't realize how striking my nose looks from the side
I've always thought the bridge was too skinny and angular
But now
Now I'm posing for my insta-story with a little more side angle
You should
You should stick with it head on really
You've got a great symmetrical thing going
Almost euro features from the front
From the side
Well
And I'm not posing with peace signs or pulling back my eyes while I
take tourist pictures in Chinatown or in front of the UN or the new Panda
Express on 9th
I'm not
Ok
I'm not
So don't
Just don't
I'm woke ok
I marched with the Women
I've protested in the
The parks
I made signs
With different colored sharpie
And even bought a nice pole
A reusable one
Because we've been making so many signs for so many protests every
other
You know
So
I *invested*

And I voted for Obama
(The second time)
And I voted for Bernie
And then Clinton
Even though
Yeah I know they're both
Fine fine fine
The point is
I'm just not into Asian guys
And I shouldn't be penalized for taste
For my opinion
For what gets my dick hard or not
And it's not about childhood conditioning
Or standards of beauty
Or internalized racism
Or or or
And you're so much hotter than my Asian friends
Trust me
So
Like
Own that
Know that
You're Way better looking than Harold Or Kumar
You're way hotter than my first roommate who was Vietnamese American
And when I write Vietnamese American or Asian American or African
American or anything that has previously been hyphenated
I Don't
Because you aren't a hyphenated people
I know that
I minored in Race and Ethnic Relations
So I don't hyphen
I'm an ally
Right

An ally

So don't go crying Wolf when I'm not swiping right on your profile

Not poking you

Not woofing at you

Not grinding up on your yellow ass at the black party

Which I go to

Cause I think the white party perpetuates color stigma

So I'm even an ally with my wallet

You know how expensive those circuit parties are

So when I say No fats femmes or Asians on my profile

Don't take it personally

It's a preference

You have preferences

Everyone does

It's the truth

It's about what I like

I take care of my body

I go to the gym

I used to be a fat kid

And you know what I did

I worked my ass off

And now

Now I'm not fat

And femme

My mom tagged me in this picture for Throwback Thursday

Which she only just discovered

And it's a picture of me as a kid

In a brown

Three piece pinstriped suit

And I'm beveling

Be-Vel-Ling

No wonder I got beat up

Called faggot and sissy growing up

Stuffed into lockers

Head swirled down the toilet

I know what oppression is

I've experienced bullying

It hurt

And I've become stronger because of it

I'm literally stronger than any of those bullies

Who are all married and miserable with multiple children from their high school sweethearts

So if I can overcome that

Then no one has an excuse to be fat or femme if they want to date me

And fat and thick and juicy are people's preferences

Great

You get off on that

You do you

Just not me

It floats someone else's boat

I'm all about that

Float it

I just have a history of heart attacks and high cholesterol in my family

So losing weight was also part of my life saving choices

Exercising my agency

You know

But you're hot for an Asian

And not fat

Your six pack looked sick in your profile

Even though I've always said six packs on skinny guys are like big tits on fat chicks

Yours looks like you worked on it

Exercised agency

And your voice is deep

That's fucking hot

And you can grow facial hair

Who knew it could grow more than a Fu Manchu stache

So

So

So I don't date Asians

But I'm going to fuck you

I'm going to make you moan like a geisha's first time

And rail you like the Transcontinental Railroad

And take you like the Rape of Nanking

Drop my load in you like we did in Hiroshima And Nagasaki

And conquer your ass like we plan to in North Korea

I also minored in Asian American history

Not cause I have yellow fever

I'm not a rice queen

I don't fuck chinks

But I'm feeling altruistic

Our zodiac signs must be ultra compatible

Was my name in your last fortune cookie?

Cause you just hit the jackpot like those Chinese ladies with clear plastic visors sitting at the slot machines in Vegas

Get your ass ready

I don't want to taste any miso soup down there

Make sure it's clean

Cause I know you're a bottom

I'll even let you be a power bottom

Cause I'm generous like that

Cause I'm a woke ally

Cause I majored in sociology

Wanna get sushi beforehand?

Daniel K. Isaac is a Korean American actor and writer born and raised in Southern California, currently based in New York City. www.DanielKIsaac.com.

The First Day Play

Abraham Johnson

CHARACTERS:

DAUGHTER

MOTHER/LISTENER/TALKER

SETTING:

Here. Now.

(MOTHER and DAUGHTER walk out onto a blank stage. DAUGHTER carries a white blanket that trails behind her.)

MOTHER Over here!

DAUGHTER Mom, hold on.

MOTHER We're going to be late.

DAUGHTER We're never late. We're slow, but we get there.

MOTHER Poetic today?

DAUGHTER Always. Always poetic.

MOTHER I raised you right.

DAUGHTER *(grunts)*

MOTHER Are you excited?

DAUGHTER No.

MOTHER ... Yay! Your first day out!

DAUGHTER Can we go back home now?

MOTHER You're going to do so many amazing things!

DAUGHTER I wanna go back to bed.

MOTHER We don't have time to sleep! Today's your day! You ate breakfast, right?

DAUGHTER Yes, Mom.

MOTHER You didn't use too much syrup, did you?

DAUGHTER Enough. I used enough, Mom.

MOTHER Good. You know how your blood pressure is.

DAUGHTER Look, I'm fine. Can we just get this over with?

MOTHER Oh. Of course. Yes. Let's go on...

DAUGHTER Mom, you promised not to get—

MOTHER Get what? I'm not getting anything! You're getting weird. Don't take your stress out on me!

(Daughter moves to hug Mother. Mother is bolstering herself.)

DAUGHTER We're almost there.

MOTHER Yeah, well... you should probably...

(Mother pulls away from Daughter)

DAUGHTER Wait, Mom?

MOTHER I wish nothing but magic for you.

(Then Mother is gone)

DAUGHTER I... forgive you.

(Daughter looks around for a moment until she finally sits down and drops the blanket in front of her. She folds it up to look as lumpy as possible. Then, she sticks out her hands— as if the blanket is a fire.)

DAUGHTER Yep. I forgive you. You know what, it's fine. Not to worry, I'm just gonna sit out here. Alone. In the wilderness. On my first day out. But I totally forgive you. No worries. Not... hello? *(Beat)* If anyone is listening, I'd like to say thank you! For listening, I mean. You don't really need to, but I appreciate it! *(Beat)* Silence is fine too! That's an acceptable response! *(Beat)* But a little noise would be—

(A loud clank comes from off stage. Following this, LISTENER enters. She

is the same actress who plays Mother. LISTENER drags behind her a large burlap bag. It looks almost as if there is a body inside it.)

LISTENER Did you say something?

DAUGHTER Yes! Hello! I appreciate you!

LISTENER Uh... you're welcome.

DAUGHTER Are you sure? I don't want you to listen if I'm not welcome.

LISTENER I suppose we've got a little time... what were you saying? Before I came here, I heard talking.

DAUGHTER Oh! Yes, I was just talking to myself.

LISTENER Do you do that often?

DAUGHTER My mom said I'm very good company.

LISTENER Where is she now?

DAUGHTER Well she... it's my first day out.

LISTENER Yeah, feels that way over here too.

DAUGHTER What? It's your first day too?

LISTENER No, that was just... wait. Your first day? You aren't joking?

DAUGHTER No. It's really my first day.

LISTENER Oh... well tell me everything!

DAUGHTER What?

LISTENER How does it feel? Have you seen anyone else yet? What does everything look like?

DAUGHTER Uh... it feels really big. You're the first person I've seen. And everything looks... bright?

LISTENER That's so— you're really lucky, kid. First day out. That's crazy.

DAUGHTER Well how long have you been out?

LISTENER I can't remember.

DAUGHTER Hmmm... I'm scared of that.

LISTENER Scared?

DAUGHTER Of not remembering.

LISTENER Oh... uh, don't cry.

DAUGHTER I'm not crying.

LISTENER *(beginning to cry gently)* Good, I just... sometimes when I hear people cry I just... oh wow, it's just a little...

DAUGHTER Whoa, okay it's— it's fine, it's going to be... do you need to sit down?

LISTENER No... no, I'm fine. I... sometimes when I listen for too long, I get a little sad. In a beautiful way.

DAUGHTER How do you mean?

LISTENER Well, it's all just so... dazzling. Bright, like you said. I forget that sometimes.

DAUGHTER My mom said it isn't always that way.

LISTENER No. It's not. It very rarely is, actually.

(Listener swings the bag and heaves a large sigh. Composed again.)

DAUGHTER That looks heavy.

LISTENER It can be... that blanket looks soft.

DAUGHTER It is.

(A beat. Daughter offers the blanket to Listener. Listener accepts it and stares intensely. Maybe she is considering taking it. After a moment, Daughter takes it back.)

DAUGHTER Well, I'm sure you've got to be on your way.

LISTENER My way? Oh... yes. It was good to meet you. Do happy things.

(Listener slowly exits with the bag.)

DAUGHTER Hmmm. That was... nice.

(She drapes the blanket around herself, tying a knot at her neck and wearing it as a cape.)

DAUGHTER First day out in the world and I've already met an entire person! I've got experiences now. DO YOU HEAR THAT MOM? EXPERI-ENCE!... whoa. Did you hear that? An echo! Hello-o-o-o! Crazy. Sound is *crazy.*

(TALKER enters. Same actress as the mother, but a slight change in costume. Maybe a scarf and glasses.)

TALKER Sound isn't crazy, actually. It's scientific.

DAUGHTER Oh, uh, hello! Who are—

TALKER You see, when we speak, we make these vibrations with our vocal chords— that's a muscle in your throat— and those produce sound waves which leave our mouth in varying strengths and accents and tones, which sound like human language. We speak English, but people everywhere speak different languages. So actually, sound isn't crazy. It's not crazy at all.

DAUGHTER Uh... thanks. Who are—

TALKER But it's not always a good thing. In fact, it's reckless to say that it's a good thing. Sound can be very bad. Terrible, actually. People turned sounds into languages billions of years ago and since then, well, you probably don't know this, but there have been terrible things! Books, writing, which lead to organization, and organization lead to politics and religion, and then we had wars and people died and after all of that, language is a pretty terrible thing. Sounds are terrible things.

(Beat. Daughter waits to see if she's going to be interrupted.)

DAUGHTER Well, I don't think sounds are bad.

TALKER What! That's wrong. You're wrong.
DAUGHTER No. Cuz I met a person before you and we talked and had a very nice conversation.

TALKER What did you talk about?

DAUGHTER Well, it's my first day out so we talked about that.

TALKER It's your first day out and you're trying to tell me what's good and what's bad?

DAUGHTER I just don't think words are bad things. I don't think sounds are—

TALKER You're being stupid. You're being stupid and childish and— of course sounds are bad things!

DAUGHTER Then why are you making them?

(Beat.)

TALKER But... that's different. I've been out longer than you. I know things.

DAUGHTER I do too.

TALKER But you, you, you, you don't! You can't. How would you know them? It's your first day out.

DAUGHTER I just do. I feel it.

TALKER Well, I *feel* that you're wrong.

DAUGHTER Well I *feel* that you should leave me alone.

TALKER Fine!

DAUGHTER Fine!

TALKER Fine!

(Talker exits, huffing. After a moment—)

DAUGHTER *(angrily)* I wish you nothing but kindness and a warm bed to share your person with!

(Beat.)

DAUGHTER Serves them right. Say I don't know about things. Making sounds is bad. Stupid. How can... *sounds... SOUNDS... words... FEEL-INGS....* yeah. *That* was so terrible *(A noise is heard offstage)* Maybe... maybe my sounds were too loud... *(She makes sure the coast is clear)* Here. Here's my contribution. And I'll do it quietly. My mom used to tell me stories when I was scared. And we'd sing together— but I'm not going to sing for you because I'm shy. Although I will tell you a story... are you ready?

(She lays the blanket down on the floor, spreading it out, and sits on it.)

DAUGHTER Once upon a time, there was a person. You were a person, let's say. Then you'll invest more in— whatever. Anyways, you were a person. And you said things. And you did things. And some of them were really, really good! And I'm proud of you for them! But some of them were very bad. Incredibly bad. Terrible, awful things. Maybe to some really good people. Or people you loved. And you felt bad about them. And you still feel bad about them. And maybe that makes you feel good sometimes, because badness can look like goodness, I think. I don't know, this whole thing is very confusing. But, anyway, you were a person who did terrible, wonderful things. And you went out one day and said, "I'm going to con- tribute!" ... probably, I don't know you very well but I can assume.

(Daughter continues, not seeing, as Mother enters again. She sits down somewhere behind Daughter, listening.)

Regardless, you probably tried to contribute, which is good, ya know? But it didn't always go according to plan. You fell in love with the right people. Maybe the wrong people. Maybe you fell in love with yourself— I truly, really hope you did. But maybe not. So after walking everywhere, after seeing everyone, after learning all the things that you thought you could know... maybe that wasn't enough for you. Maybe... maybe you're still looking. I don't know what for. Maybe... maybe you don't want to know. That can be a bit easier sometimes, right?...
But after everything, after you spent all your time up and did what you could to learn and say and do all the things you did... you stopped looking. You stopped needing to know the answer. You stopped asking why you did those terrible wonderful things. Stopped blaming yourself or exalting yourself... and decided to love yourself and all those around you. You thanked them for being wonderful, terrible people. Fiercely and

radically, you held a fear of yourself in your hand and prayed for it: "I wish you nothing but kindness and a warm bed to share your person with… I'm sure you've got to be on your way."

(Daughter stands and picks the blanket up— still not seeing Mother.)

DAUGHTER Well, that was a crazy story, right! I guess sounds really are weird!

(From her spot on the floor, Mother begins to clap. Daughter jumps, then sees her.)

DAUGHTER Mom! What are you doing here?!

(Mother says nothing, but smiles at Daughter. Maybe they hug.)

DAUGHTER Mom, you can't believe the things that I've seen today! First, there was this person who came and they carried this really heavy thing and we had a very nice conversation. And after that, I met this other person who wasn't really as nice and kept correcting me and I didn't really like that… but then I made up a story! And I told it! And then I ran into you! I've missed you a lot!

(Mother doesn't say anything. She nods along with her Daughter.)

DAUGHTER Mom? Is something wrong?

(Mother shakes her head, smiling. After a moment, she pulls Daughter in for a hug. She holds her tightly.)

DAUGHTER Mom? That kind of hurts.

(Mother releases. Daughter sits back on the floor staring.)

DAUGHTER You... something's wrong.

(Mother smiles, but nods.)

DAUGHTER I... can I go home with you tonight?

(Mother shakes her head.)

DAUGHTER Oh... when can I come back?

(Mother smiles, but makes no indication. Daughter takes a moment to understand, but when she does, she gathers up her blanket. She lifts it, draping it around mother. When she does so Mother smiles at her, and gives her one last hug. Finally, Mother exits, wrapped in the blanket. Daughter watches her go. A long beat.)

DAUGHTER I wish you nothing but kindness.

(Lights down. End of play.)

Abraham Johnson is a writer from Rome, Georgia who enjoys sleeping, any kind of cheese, and being friends with incredible playwrights (thanks Lambda!). His work has been developed around the South with the Horizon Theater, Out of Box Theater, Lionheart Theater, Sundress Academy for The Arts, and the New Georgia Group.

Bango Shank, Kid Detective
Calvin Kasulke

A high school science classroom, present day.

In the center of the classroom lies a body, motionless. The
body wears an unhip shirt tucked into unhip khakis.

Two NERDS loiter beside the corpse.

Enter BANGO SHANK, KID DETECTIVE. He
approaches the teens and the corpse.

NERD THE FIRST

Thank god you're here.

NERD THE SECOND

There is no god.

BANGO

Let's cut to the chase.

Bango inspects the corpse.

NERD THE FIRST

What had happened was we were trying to cook up something that would get you just like, mega-high when you huffed it but when we came in here to ask Mr. Pearson for some more ammonia he was just like, all cold and on the floor and shit—

NERD THE SECOND

See existence is just this totally arbitrary thing and with no way to measure objective reality we can conclude consciousness is an illusion at best and at worst just this total
bummer like who even asked for this—

BANGO

He's dead.

NERD THE FIRST

Oh man.

NERD THE SECOND

You see why we called you.

NERD THE FIRST

Science club can't afford getting written up again.

NERD THE SECOND

Not after the tactical marinara thing last month --

BANGO

This is probably a violation of the code of conduct.

NERD THE FIRST

They'll cancel the club.

NERD THE SECOND

I need this for my college application.

BANGO

I'm on it. Where's the lab room?

NERD THE FIRST

Right in there.

BANGO

I'll take a look around.

NERD THE FIRST

Thank you.

> Bango exits. For a beat, the nerds loiter alone. Enter
> FURGIS TURGIS, KID DETECTIVE. Furgis crosses to
> the body.

NERD THE FIRST

Thank god you're here.

NERD THE SECOND

Is there a god?

FURGIS

What's the situation?

NERD THE FIRST

We found him.

FURGIS

He's dead.

NERD THE SECOND

We can't let the science club take the blame.

FURGIS

Of course not.

NERD THE SECOND	FURGIS
The tactical marinara incident.	The tactical marinara incident.

Furgis stands up from examining the unhip corpse.

NERD THE FIRST

What do we do?

FURGIS

It might have something to do with the chemicals in the lab — it's through there?

Furgis exits. The nerds loiter. Enter ARMANI BAPTISE, KID DETECTIVE.

NERD THE FIRST

Thank god.

NERD THE SECOND

Who?

ARMANI

Dead?

NERD THE FIRST

Who?

ARMANI

God.

NERD THE SECOND

Yes.

ARMANI

Good. Him?

NERD THE FIRST

Also.

ARMANI

Got it.

NERD THE SECOND

Please help. Our club can't --

NERD THE FIRST	ARMANI
The marinara.	The marinara.

NERD THE SECOND

Exactly.

ARMANI

The lab?

NERD THE FIRST

Through there.

ARMANI

Perfect.

> Armani exits. The nerds loiter. Enter Bango Shank, Kid Detective.

NERD THE FIRST

Did you find any clues?

NERD THE SECOND

Do you know how he died?

NERD THE FIRST

Can you prove it wasn't our fault?

BANGO

Listen up. The evidence, as I have gathered and reasoned, is as follows --

> Enter FURGIS.

FURGIS

Aha! The criminal always returns to the scene of the crime.

BANGO

So you're turning yourself in.

FURGIS

You're under arrest.

BANGO

You're thirteen.

FURGIS

Twelve.

BANGO

So you admit it.

Enter Armani.

As this continues, the two nerds pick up the corpse. They exit, carrying the body into the lab room.

ARMANI

The criminal!

FURGIS

Who?

NERD THE SECOND

God.

ARMANI

Who?

BANGO

Aha, an accomplice.

ARMANI

Where?

FURGIS

I knew I'd find you here.

BANGO

It was all part of my plan.

ARMANI

Busted.

Enter the two nerds, followed by the body — an unhip, undead MR. PEARSON. Mr. Pearson is covered in marinara sauce.

BANGO

He's alive?

FURGIS

How?

ARMANI

God?

NERD THE SECOND

Nooo.

NERD THE FIRST

Nothing like that.

NERD THE SECOND

We finally found a use for // the marinara.

BANGO, FURGIS AND ARMANI

The marinara.

FURGIS

Of course.

BANGO

I knew it.

ARMANI

Elementary!

A beat. What now?

BANGO

Well then, I guess...

ARMANI

Case closed.

BANGO

That's right.

FURGIS

Another successful investigation for Furgis Turgis, Kid Detective.

BANGO

I think you mean: Just one more mystery solved by Bango Shank, Kid
Detective.

The detectives look at Armani expectantly.

ARMANI

Did you all do the math homework?

The BELL RINGS.

END OF PLAY.

Calvin Kasulke is a playwright living in Brooklyn, NY.

Maybe Politics Are Over
an excerpt
Sloka Krishnan

CHARACTERS

four POLITICIANS:

    THE POWERFUL ONE

    THE BEAUTIFUL ONE

    THE INCOMPETENT ONE

    THE TRUE BELIEVER

a TRIO OF WEIRDOS

three WOMEN

SCENE 1

(*A men's bathroom. One stall, one urinal. The stall has no door. THE POW-ERFUL ONE sits on the closed toilet lid. He looks a mess. He is drunk. He is drinking. THE BEAUTIFUL ONE walks in and begins to piss. He doesn't see THE POWERFUL ONE, but THE POWERFUL ONE sees him, in the mirror. He begins to speak, startling THE BEAUTIFUL ONE mid-stream.*)

THE POWERFUL ONE

Take it from me, kid: You be a man out there, yeah? You be the most beautiful fucking man, yeah? Successful, bold, a real charmer. And then over here: You get your dick fuckin hard, you fuck who you want, you fuck how you want, when you want, you name it. Whatever kinky shit your heart desires. A man like you, that face, that fuckin suit, that fuckin body, you go into a meeting and you can lay your fucking cock right on the goddamn conference table, you hear me? You lay your cock on that table I guarantee you in five seconds everyone around leans over to suck it. Swear to God.

You're rock hard in two minutes, cumming all over their pretty little faces, swear to God.

I used to do it, go into the fucking board room like that. You think it's a metaphor? It's not a metaphor. I used to—still could, still could get assholes like you—like all of them—fucking salivating over this shit if the fucking President hadn't decided to sabotage his—his best fucking shot at a competent administration.

You ever sucked a dick? The gays, man, that's the one thing they've got figured out, the fuckin power of a hard dick.

If I could suck my own cock I would, lemme tell ya. You say solipsism; I say fuckin … self-reliance. Self-sufficiency. Freedom! You ever see someone suck his own cock? Go online and look that shit up. That's my advice to you. Man at his fucking finest.

SCENE 2

(In a different place, a TRIO OF WEIRDOS sing a song.)

THE WEIRDOS
There's a little log cabin by a river
and a sprinkling of freshly-fallen snow;
there's the bright glare of sunlight in the morning
in this place we found so many years ago.

In this place we found so many years ago,
there are things we never knew that there could be:
things like funguses and poisons and all sorts of odd debris,
things like somehow for the first time feeling free.

And the bears that share the forest are majestic and so strong,
and utopia was quietly domestic all along,
and we were foolish in the city, we were foolish in the throng,
but now we're here, but now we're here:

With a little log cabin by a river,

with a sprinkling of freshly-fallen snow,

with the bright glare of sunlight in the morning,

and with more and more and more of this to go.

SCENE 3

(WOMEN 1 AND 2 at a café. Aside, THE INCOMPETENT ONE stands at a podium and speaks into a microphone.)

THE INCOMPETENT ONE

On behalf of the White House, I hereby declare that women are fucking vile. Truly disgusting. Thank you.

WOMAN 1:	Well, this man is awful.
WOMAN 2:	So bad.
WOMAN 1:	Women are not disgusting.
WOMAN 2:	Women are excellent!
WOMAN 1:	I hate this man.
WOMAN 2:	He is horrible. We should get rid of him.
WOMAN 1:	You know who else is bad?
WOMAN 2:	Who?
WOMAN 1:	Trans women.
WOMAN 2:	So bad.
WOMAN 1:	The worst.
WOMAN 2:	Tell me about it.

(WOMAN 3 walks in.)

WOMAN 3:   This man is horrible.
Since I have had a vagina since birth, mine is the correct opinion. Am I right?

WOMAN 1:   What a good and logical criterion that doesn't at all reduce women to their reproductive and/or sexual capacity!

WOMAN 2:   We should codify it for sure.

WOMAN 3:   We are very good feminists. Look at this cute button I have!

ALL: Hashtag resistance!

                (They take a selfie.)

SCENE 4

(The bathroom. THE BEAUTIFUL ONE rolls in the window, trying to be sneaky, obviously failing. He sits on the toilet seat and practices his Wide Stance. Tentatively tapping a foot closer to the edge of the stall. Tentatively reaching a hand down, under the divider, imagining holding a penis. It is only a practice environment, of course, since there isn't even a second stall, much less another man. But he is very focused. And shockingly vulnerable! He closes his eyes and touches himself through his pants. The door opens, and he hurriedly stops.)

THE POWERFUL ONE

I knew you were a dirty motherfucker! Enjoying yourself, huh? Don't let me stop you, I'm just here to piss.

                (He starts pissing, enthusiastically.)

Better your hand than a fucking pussy these days, I tell you what. More trouble than it's worth. Girls'll beg for your dick and then head straight to the press to lie about it. Or they'll cling. Jesus! If there's one thing I can't stand it's a clingy bitch. Fuck! My dick is shriveling just thinking about it. Fuckin hell.

                (He finishes.)

Come on then, whip it out, you don't have all day.

(He winks and leaves. THE BEAUTIFUL ONE hesitates, then does as instructed and comes hard.)

SCENE 5

(The café and podium again.)

THE INCOMPETENT ONE

Also on behalf of the President, we can't friggin wait until these smug liberal assholes lose their health coverage.

WOMAN 1:   What a monster.

WOMAN 2:   Hideous.

WOMAN 1:   This is a death sentence for so many people!

WOMAN 2:   Unbelievably cruel.

WOMAN 1:   Well, I guess the idiots who voted for him will finally get what they deserve.

(The two laugh uproariously and maliciously.)

WOMAN 2:   They'll weed out the narrow-minded losers, that's for sure.

(WOMAN 3 walks in.)

WOMAN 3:   My God. You saw the news?

WOMAN 1:   We did.

WOMAN 2:   Horrible! Just horrible!

WOMAN 3:   These evil sons of bitches won't be so smug when half their base is wiped out.

WOMAN 2:   That's what I said!

ALL: Good riddance!

(They cackle some more.)

SCENE 6

(THE TRUE BELIEVER addresses the Senate.)

THE TRUE BELIEVER

You know, I had a dream last night. And in it, all of us were here, in this chamber, and all of us were One with Christ. All of us! Even you, Senator, even you. Ha! But jokes aside, let me tell you, this unity was ... profound. And filled with truth. Christ was within us all, moving us for the good of this Nation that has been moving away from Him for too long. Christ was within us and He spoke, He shared with us the promise of a beautiful and righteous Christian nation with a pure heart and a strong moral core. Senators, this is the Nation that it is our duty to create. A Nation that leaves forever the path of immorality and sin down which it has strayed and chooses instead immortality, eternal life in Christ, in His beauty, in His power, in His overwhelming grace. That is where our country is headed: to the joy and glory of living in Christ. Our duty is to usher in this era.

But Mr. Vice President, you say. How do we do this when so many among us are weak, are sinful, when so many among us willfully disregard the blessing that has been offered to us in Christ?

Let me tell you how I had this dream.

I was in bed last night. I was in bed, and next to me my wife slept soundly, but I could not sleep. The future of this country weighed heavily on my mind. In order to lift the weight, I thought of turning to ... idleness, distraction. To the sin of self-gratification. I admit that. I admit my imper-fection. But the strength of Christ allowed me to turn away from this and to turn to Him instead. And I submitted myself in prayer, reaching out to Christ, seeking His love, sharing with Him my worries and fears.

And He responded. Christ came to my bed and asked, my child, why you are suffering? And His presence soothed me. I felt a great warmth that began in my heart and spread through my body. My skin felt so sensitive to the sheets. My breathing grew deeper, heavier. My eyelids grew heavy. My whole being was undulating, relaxing as it hadn't been able to in weeks. And then the warmth grew, roaring, into a fire, and I was vibrating, and Christ was showing me His power, showing me the power of our union. My throat was constricted, my body struggled to move up, up to meet Him. In the light behind my eyelids I saw his figure, illuminated, and I felt my tongue reach out unbidden, this muscle stretching to salve his holy wounds. Their taste of iron and salt was real, and it was painful, and I was overcome with emotion, overcome by Christ's beauty and generosity, overcome by His love, overcome by the intimacy and freedom with which He gives that love.

I didn't know that the heat could grow stronger but it did, and it continued to pulse within me with ever-greater intensity, and I was shaking then, and Christ was in front of me, holding me, and inside me, inside me and filling me wholly, leaving no room for doubt, leaving no room for anything but faith in His love. And we were together imbued with

Krishnan

a searing light that grew brighter and brighter, and I clung to Him, fearful, I clung to His pain, which was my pain, I reached for His wounds, which were my wounds, I couldn't stand it anymore, I didn't know what He was doing, but I trusted Him, I cried out, I am sure, cried out His name over and over until my throat was raw, until my voice was brittle, and then—

Like piercing daybreak, like a revelation, like water bursting forth from behind a dam, the light and the heat shattered into glorious flames, Christ shattered into flames, I shattered into flames, and there was no more pain, there was no more worry, there was nothing but waves and waves and waves of the most ineffable bright and crackling beauty.

I don't know how long I rode these waves. When they finally subsided, my limbs were weak, my bed saturated with sweat, my pillow flooded by tears I did not know I had shed. I was broken, more fully surrendered to Christ than perhaps ever before. And a great peace washed over me.

And then I slept. And then, Senators, I had this beautiful dream, with all of you. And we all felt this same full surrender, we all felt our desires satiated and our bodies healed by Christ. He alone will do this for us and for this country.

This is why, good Senators, I will be voting "no" on this wasteful bill, should a tiebreak be necessary. I urge you to reject it outright.

SCENE 7

THE WEIRDOS

We saw Bigfoot in the forest; he was gentle, he was dreaming,
he was splashing in a stream, and he was singing to himself.

We saw Bigfoot; he was wearing a nice skirt he'd made from grass,
and as we passed, he smiled a smile that made our hearts beat extra fast.

And then we said:
Excuse me, sir, we couldn't help but notice
your pretty eyes, your joyful voice!

And then he said:
I'm grateful that you're here and that you noticed.
Come down and join me, and let's rejoice in that we've found each other
now!

Oooh-ooh-ooh! Oooh-ooh-ooh! And we rejoiced!

We met Bigfoot in the forest, and we held each other tight,
and it felt right, and other animals came down and joined the love.

And we were underneath the moonlight; we were underneath the stars,
and our guitar's reverberation felt like wisdom from afar.

And then we danced!
And celebrated life and coexistence!
And we felt young, and we felt proud.

And as we danced,
humanity receded in the distance.
But in its wake it left a cloud of dust that settled on us all.

We found Bigfoot in the forest; he was prancing, he was twirling;
we were swirling through a place that we all longed to call our home.

But the home was an illusion; as we swayed under the eaves
and felt the leaves crunch underfoot, we knew: simplicity deceives.

Sloka Krishnan is a playwright-lyricist interested in magic; extravagance; ritual; and the disavowal of moral purity and coherent identity. In the DC area, his plays have received readings by the Rainbow Theatre Project and as a part of Forum Theatre (Re)Acts, and he is a 2017-2018 Playwright Apprentice at Horizon Theatre in Atlanta.

Buddy
an excerpt
Michael Shayan

ACT I

Scene One

A picnic table in a New York City park. SAM sits alone, his face lit by the
moon and his laptop screen. He's typing, drinking a BIG GULP and eating
sour cream and onion CHIPS.

ZEKE (O.S.)

I WOULD GO OUT TONIGHT
BUT I HAVEN'T GOT A STITCH TO WE-EA-AR
THIS MAN SAID IT'S GRUESOME
THAT SOMEONE HMM HMM HMMM

Sam notices, lights a cigarette and goes back to work.

ZEKE approaches a nearby tree. He takes a wide stance, unzips and pees.
He slaps the tree with his palm.

ZEKE

Fuck!

He finishes and hops on the bench. He doesn't notice Sam.

He taps a pack of cigarettes against his palm several times and sticks one in his mouth.

ZEKE

Bad bad bad bad bad bad bad bad this is bad this is really really bad
this is fuck this is bad this is fucked this is fucking FUCK where the fuck
is my –

He searches his pockets for a lighter.

SAM

Hey, man, are you, uh –

ZEKE

She tried to fucking kill herself! She she she she she did it right there
right fucking there right in front of me looking at me dead dead dead in
the eyes she did it she tried it she tried to do it and and and I left I left I
left her there I fucking left I fuck I I I I I – buddy, buddy, you got a light?

Sam tosses him a WHITE LIGHTER. Zeke tosses it back.

ZEKE

What the fuck! What the fuck, buddy! You trying to fucking kill me?
Great. Great, great. Great! (Mumbles) It's like I don't even know why
they make 'em, it's it's it's STUPID stupid and –

SAM

What? What? I don't –

ZEKE

I mean are you fucking stupid, buddy? Bad luck. No good. White lighters
are fucked! (Pause) This fuckin' guy –

SAM

Sorry, what? Wait, why?

ZEKE

Wait why what?

SAM

Why are they bad luck?

ZEKE

Why are they – don't fucking ask me that, man, how would I know why something / is –

SAM

Hey, are you – Do you, uh, want some ice, or – (offering the Big Gulp) this is a Diet Coke, or –

ZEKE

Diet Coke? No I don't want Diet Coke, I want a fucking LIGHT, a light, a lighter, I mean fuck, I – here, can I –

Zeke leans over and lights his cigarette off of Sam's. He takes a long puff.

ZEKE

Whew! Good looking out, buddy. (Pause) I'm good. I'm cool. (Pause) FUCK! I'm cool. I'm cool.

Sam tries to go back to what he was doing. Zeke is cool.

Zeke notices that his fly is open. He zips up and sticks out his hand.

ZEKE

I'm Zeke!

Sam stares at the hand and shakes, tentatively.

SAM

Sam.

Scene Two

SAM sits at the bench, reading and snacking on CHIPS. It's quiet.

We hear footsteps. Sam recognizes the sound and quickly hides the chips.

RACHEL makes a dramatic entrance wearing big sunglasses, a hat, a free
"New Yorker" tote ... she throws her bag onto the table.

RACHEL

Guess who's gay?

SAM

Oh, I love this game and I have absolutely no idea.

RACHEL

Just take a guess, take a wild / guess.

SAM

Guess, I can't just guess, like I need clues, like is he tall, is he hot, is he
your tall hot cousin Dave 'cause if he is I definitely told you so?

She washes down a pill with a big bottle of Evian.

RACHEL

It's Axel. Axel's gay now.

SAM

Axel The German With The Big Dick?

RACHEL

Axel The German With The Big Dick is gay. And I mean it is just beyond – I mean we used to fuck, like really, seriously fuck, and now he's taken off to Tonga with his Puerto Rican lover Javier. I mean my God, what a waste.

SAM

Oh, my God, that's crazy! Can I have his number?

RACHEL

And of course I found out on my way to therapy, which was very unfortunate because I had so much to cover with Dr. Stein and all we talked about was Axel the G with the big D. Ugh, my life is so hopeless! (Pause) And how are you, Samuel?

SAM

Oh, fine, I'm fine. Never better!

RACHEL
(Sniffing)
Something smells onion-y. (Pause) Sour cream and onion-y.

SAM

Don't look at me...

RACHEL

Hey, so how'd it go with Travis?

SAM

It didn't. He canceled last minute.

RACHEL

Oh, weird.

SAM

It's fine, though. Like I'm totally over it.

RACHEL

Well, thank God for that. Because I mean he was so much cuter in high school and he still wears Lacoste.

SAM

Yeah. It's just like bizarre, you know, like I thought we had a great first date, like we had chemistry, / and –

RACHEL

But like it wasn't really a date though, right? Like I mean I thought you guys were just like "catching up" over coffee / or whatever.

SAM

Yeah, so? You've never had a coffee date?

RACHEL

I mean yeah but it just seems like more of like a friendly get-together.

SAM

Okay, so why would he sit there for like five or six hours laughing at my jokes and like letting me pay the bill if he wasn't, like, into me, or like / trying to –

RACHEL

Because you were getting together. To catch-up. During the day.

Shayan

SAM

Whatever. I'm over it.

                                                              A pause.

RACHEL

So, did / you hear about –

SAM

Should I text him? I should text / him –

RACHEL

No, no, not happening.

SAM

Why? Why can't I just –

RACHEL

Because you sound very desperate right now and it's very unattractive.

SAM
(à la Bette Davis)

But I am, Rachel! I am desperate!

RACHEL

Calm down, Baby Jane. I mean I don't know what to tell you. You keep going after these guys that are just, like – I don't know. I don't know. (Pause)
And I'm sorry but you're just acting like such a victim / when it's like –

SAM

What? What're you –

RACHEL

I mean it's like you totally ghosted my friend Mark, / poor thing, and –

SAM

I did not "ghost" him, okay?

RACHEL

You said you were going to the bathroom and left the bar.

SAM

No…! *(Pause)* Well, yeah. Yeah. *(Pause)* In my defense, I did kinda have to pee.

RACHEL

And I mean he was like super into you, and –

SAM

And super not my type.

RACHEL

Well okay but I mean at least he was like in the same league.

A pause.

RACHEL

That came out wrong.

SAM

Okay.

RACHEL

You know I didn't mean it that way. I just think you know exactly what's going on and what you need to do to / get guys to, like –

SAM

And we're not doing this.

RACHEL

Okay, well we don't have to do this, but don't act like you don't know. Because you know.

SAM

Yeah, I know, I'm a big fat guy, okay? And I love chips. So let's move on!

A long pause.

SAM

Do you think I'm depressed?

RACHEL

I mean probably.

SAM

No, really.

RACHEL

Yeah, really. I mean I think most people are depressed. So does Gloria.

SAM

Right. I was gonna ask, how's she / doing with –

RACHEL

How do you *think* she's doing, Sam? I mean she's never been alone a day in her life. My father's off in the middle of *(mocking Gloria)* "God knows

where doing God knows what to who," and so of course I have to drive
her to meet with the lawyers, and her yoga teacher and various medical
professionals, and – *(Pause)* And it's selfish, really. And I mean now I have
to adjust my entire life because they couldn't stick it out a few more years.

SAM
(To himself)

Yeah, and I'm the victim.

RACHEL

Excuse me?

SAM

Nothing.

A long pause.

SAM

Have you been writing?

RACHEL

Were you not listening to anything I just said? I haven't had time to
breathe, you think I've had / time to think about –

SAM

I'm just asking.

RACHEL

Yeah, well, don't.

Sam gets up and starts to leave.

SAM

I gotta go, I have / to work on this –

RACHEL

No, don't. I'm sorry. *(Pause)* Come on, sit. Sam, I'm –

He sits. A pause.

SAM

So, what're you gonna do? About Axel.

RACHEL

Well, there's kind of nothing to do, except for drink heavily and like wish him luck, you know? Ya hear that, Gloria – I turned another one.

SAM

Yeah. It's like all the good gay men are assholes –

RACHEL

And all the good straight ones are gay.

Scene Three

Night. Sam is at the bench alone. He's drinking a beer, snacking on chips and texting.

Zeke is by the tree, smoking and talking on the phone. He's all cleaned up.

Zeke hangs up and joins Sam on the bench. Sam turns.

SAM

Uh, hey…!

ZEKE

You sure I didn't like cuss you out or something? Cause I've definitely done that.

SAM

Yeah, no. No.

A long pause.

ZEKE

So is this happening for a reason?

SAM

What?

ZEKE

This. You and me sitting here talking. Is it happening for a reason?

SAM

Uh –

ZEKE

Someone said everything happens for a reason.

SAM

Right...

ZEKE

Someone said everything happens for a reason and then someone tried to kill herself in front of me and said I was the reason.

SAM

Oh.

A long pause.

ZEKE

It's weird, isn't it? I mean outta all the benches in the park, I pick this one,
y'know?

SAM

It's a good bench.

ZEKE

Like you could leave. You could get up right now and leave and then it'd
be over.

SAM

That's unlikely.

ZEKE

Or I could stab you. I could stab you and then it'd be like that play – that
play by that guy –

SAM

Yeah…

ZEKE

I could stab you and then I could stab myself and then it'd really be over.
Isn't that fucked up but also beautiful and kind of exciting? *(Pause. He
laughs)* Your face! Your face right now! Chill out, buddy. I'm not gonna
fuckin' stab you! *(Pause)* But I could though. I totally could.

Michael Shayan is an Iranian-American Jewish playwright and 2017 Lambda Fellow based in New York. His work has been presented or developed at The Lark, Dixon Place's HOT! Festival, Lambda Literary, LaMaMa (December 2017) and Harvard University, where he studied playwriting with mentors Sam Marks and Liz Duffy Adams.

thenamelesscity
Carlos Sirah

(0,0)   The city is dying.   (0,0)
everyThingchanges

(0,100) The city is dead.   (0,100)
everythingChanges

(0,1000) The new city./No new cities.
Everythingchanges/everythingchanges
(0,1000)

Waaaaaaaaaaaaaaaaaaaaaaaaaaaar is over!
(0,0)

When the city is dead! (0,100)

Do not cut that child in half!/Run it
through with a sword! (0,1000)

our bodies extended across gulfs of var-
ied distances, and our bodies stretched
to the limits of themselves and sometimes
past the limits and snapped or were
severed at the precipices and became a
part of the
below then reaching out of an abyss
some bodies were so light they drifted
from the planes of earth like most words
do   and like those hands that
reached form below
so too did hands reach from the above
downward bodies hands   the words
reaching from all directions toward that
center and so was the gulf between above
and below born, that old world and the
next a new directiona new abyss -from our
origins(0,1000)

-on branta nigricans-
the migration of sound from subject to
object they called out to each other to us
even in the night marking their way
        beneath a nimbus   in a lane of
the sky   belonging only to

themselves   these geese   certain of
their direction they were hunted from
below one by one   they did fall
the shape of the letter V in crisis
shattering the skein
every shot from the below
a death knell   each
different   the bodies in flight   the wings
dancing   the long fall. (0,100)

Coda: they reformed along the like lines
and trajectories in the shape of that perfect letter, V, across the dark night sky.

Love
What is what always will be.
Its shape and manifestations are differ-
ent in every age.
Exigencies of terrain, of memory,

War
If we kill the way we do war, where
does the war go?
Into what other corridors of the body,
the earth, the mind, does it burrow?

Spirit
        when the tangibles are made
scant and scarce, specificity wants to
dissolve itself, just like that. give up the
body. cause sometimes you only have
that which is inside like, my own mirror
now, the man you call my lover, for
example, what is he, is he a he? i take a
whole body of indecision and i leave you
not with myself but with a many-limbed
creature so I'm not left with one decision,
but many outcomes…
        there have been other mir-
rors, other shapes, i know, some even like
myself, and when i saw myself in a mirror
that was too much like myself so much

that the reflection, i thought, looked more like me, than me, i ran far and long, and away danger. sometimes, at night, i wonder what is a man? a woman, a human, even? let me

be clear. i will not count on your words. what good is any word right now would you tell me your whole life, not so much by the words, but by accumulation, by constellation, by parallax even, by light speak, by your relationship to light?

TIME
Heretical Lecturers, The Lovers, Holy Folks, Warriors, The Suicide Box

We decided that we would not perish. That we will not perish. That we will remember and not forget, and so time will take us. The past is continuous. So that we will not forget and remember. This is wrestling with Time. There are those among you, who cannot remember. But we will remember together. And it requires the body. All of our bodies. All of our wills. If not, then what? War. More war? (0,0)

Disaster appears. Surveys.
Does not speak. Haggard. Clothes hanging off. Singed by fire. Hair matted. Staff as long the body. Walks through from post to post to citadel to citadel to town to town through time. Surveys all which is in the space. Looks to see the people in the space. Looks into them. Looks into their spaces. Finds one who is ancestor. Reaches out the decrepit hand. Curiosity. Touch. Amusement.
Touch. Cackle.
Touch. Guffaw. Touch. Sadness.
Touch. What profound sadness!
Looks into their sadness. Sees it.
Knows that this sadness, all these sadnesses produced The Sadness.
Cannot help but weep. Tires of

weeping. Walks out of the space weeping. No. Runs back into the space. Wild. Finds the ancestor then howls and howls and howls. One wish: To reach back. To warn of the havoc. Here the theater recognizes itself. Disaster sees across storms and into the heart of time. The veil in this place, this theater, is thinner, more porous tonight, and so she howls again. It is the ugliest sound ever heard. Does it reach her great (how many greats?) grandparent. She disappears into the night. (0,0,100,1000)

Agita and Memory

The Theater. Citizens enter. Some sit. Someone climbs. Some put on goggles. Those who don't put on the goggles, watch. The goggles produce images that the audience may see via projection. The body takes on the horror of these years past. Foreground and Background. It is at once an act of memorializing, and at the same time an act of liberation. We pass through Time. Sometimes bodies get stuck in gesture. This is agita. And the person must rest. The body tries harder and harder to get out of agita only to move on to the next image. When this happens, a witness removes the goggles. The assemblage should become a visual cacophony of our past horrors. This should go on some time. Now the sonic escapes the bodies. It's a kind of church Or an anti-church. People slowly release themselves from these images and move from there into immediate joy. Now all can go to the festival. (0,1000)

The Lovers
Do you know what a doorbell is?

Would you kill me? Silence.
Would you? Silence.
No. no.....

I wanted to go with you. You say that.

Do you believe there were slaves? Yes.

Don't grab me like that.
Do it like this.

I want to destroy something. Kill yourself.

Leave here and go where?
How do you know they even dance?

Wanna make something?
If you're for real.

Eat the sun
Open the sky. (0,100)

Warriors WARRIORS warriors

Year (0,0)- The Migrations
The city is actually dead, though no one
knows it. The longest war is now over.

The sky fell. People are just flat out tired.
Even those born under the signs of war.
The Ares , mufuckers born on Thursdays,
those whose father's blood loved war.
All the war gods, are sated, And so the
peoples take their arms and bury them
deep under the ground. Some think to
smelt the aluminum, iron, and carbon
and to erect a grand monument, but they
can no longer find any good architects,
the visionaries and dreamers too are
tired and so they resign themselves to
keep the weapons out of sight. "That's a
good as anything." "If we can't see them,
we don't have to think about them."
and "Whoever thought this was a good
idea?"
    There is celebration. Cele-
bration turns into frustration from scant
resources. So we watch the city die in the
lives and minds as they grapple to come
to terms with the new condition. People
leave to escape the sun. But people are
dying, the sun is brighter, more deadly.
A cancer sweeps the nations. They begin
to see a way to live like this. Some value
of course. This nation or this village. Bor-
ders of the long wars have realigned the
world. Darkness takes the land. Actual
darkness.

Year (0,100)-Settlement
But for so many years they only for they
could only just gaze upon one another.
For many years the eyes gravitated to-
wards the ground, so strong was the pull
of the weapons, but gradually after over
a century, they began to feel their bodies
again. Instead of the ground, their eyes
craved the flesh of those around them.
The life span of people has decreased
by 20 years. A dilemma, protect the
settlements, or let people in. A person
is sent as emissary to other settlements.
Knowing that they will never ever return
to this home. The arrival of a

*stranger from somewhere else. Boon or
doom?*

The Box
What's in the box?
Air.
Just air.
Just air.
What are you doing with the air?
I'mgoingtochargeitwithadream. I
have a bigger box.
That's good for you.
My box is the perfect size I
also have a box.
That's cool.
I have a shinier box.
That's great for you.
My box doesn't need to be shiny.
where'dyougetthebox?
I made it.
When did you learn to carpenter?
Here and there, between deaths.
I thought i'd build myself a box,
I could capture a bad dream.
What if we built a big box?
Could it capture all the bad dreams?
When I said capture bad dreams,
That was a euphemism.
So if that's not what it's for, then what
we're using it for, then...
Suicide
What?
It's a suicide box.
Like a metaphysical death?
Yes
Oh ok.
Well, no.
A metaphysical death, sure.
But I'm notput limitson mybox
Oh.

The box is an object like any other.
Sure it is a box.
Encounter it, and make a choice.
See the box, say no, not death today.
Or yes death, today.
All the deaths today.
That's not funny.
I'll have some of that, death. Is it a
church?
It is not.
But it is a place.

X and Y carry a box and put it into the
center of town.
X and Y leave the center.
Z appears and examines the box.

This is a beginning:
X and Y come back and measure the
box. X determines the box lacks height.
Y determines the box is too tall.

a: take it down another inch. b: go over
it again
a: no, more than an inch by a foot, or a
cubit.
b. A cubit?
a: Yes, a cubit
b: What's a cubit?

You should try it.
Get inside.
No you try it.
You built it.
Go ahead,
Kill yourself. (0, 100)

Sirah

A Over/Heard History

And before that our people lived
on the edge, or not on the edge, in the
margin, pushed behind a thin and invisible line. The line itself more impression
but the weight was not insignificant. So
you could call it a weighted line. A pressure border, and so we were pressed
and pressed until there was an explo-
sion. And explosions begat explosions.
Not in the ways in which those who
pushed us had ever thought to conceive,
They had genocidal tendencies. Erasure
was the principal project. Amnesia its
symptom. The ability to always forget
and invent. Their complacency, the condition of power at bay. Their natural resting place. A disposition in repose could
only respond. Now let me tell you about
this thinking. Thinking happens along a
line that is continuous and it runs, and
so when we fell across the border, they
still sat. Some of them. Some of the more
liberal among them. didn't even know
what to do. So they listened to radios
and read papers, while the world around
them burned. It was sufficient for them
to mark the noise, to mark the deaths, to
mark the genocides with the prattle of
conversation.

Lovers

You don't look at me the same anymore.
There's an emptiness.
It's the same.
No it's like. I don't know what it's like I
just know it's alien.
Don't say that.
That you're an alien.
You might as well be a stranger. You get
that?

It means I don't feel anything for you.
That is something. (0,0)

Holy Folks

tell me
what is home?
home is here.
what is the past?
past is here.
are we dead?
no the city is
and time?
here and dead.
we are dead
is this a dead time?
do you speak? what
is invention here is
home failure
you are a silo
you say this
yes I say it.
and the festival
there is such thing
there is a festival
what is a thing
a festival is a thing
what is the severity
they
pillaged and raped
conquered and robbed.
they have not found us.
we hid.
that is the past.
what will happen when we find
exile
we sent them into exile
we did not send them
exiled themselves and the exiles found
each who sent them
miseries
the sun
 power.
and what about darkness?

Sirah

It is round.
is their virtue in not knowing?
there is
what of power?
it cannot be avoided.
in these circumstances
tell me.
can we speak.
never in the town.
then where
never in the city.
always in public.
are we not the public. yes.
no.
what is god
that is not the question.
don't laugh.
heretic.
why is god so oily?
heretic.

SUN

Leaps and valleys and ice that burns.
Men and women and men and men and
people of all shades and walked to the
festival They went to watch the immolation of the ones to give themselves up to
sacrifice. As was preached. If you want
to live among us. Then this is what is
required. The Rite of the Sun. The fact is
that we found ourselves as the Inheritors
of this Earth. Some would call us Meek,
but we do not accept this designation.
We do not know if this is true. WE are designed to know appreciate the breadth
of reality of existence. The material and
the immaterial alike. We do not privilege
either. We recognize the essences, the
urges as designated to us by the Children of Bessie. That the body is real and
not an abstraction. That we will always
dance. But we recognize also that with
this knowledge, we must know

how to remember. Give us the child! We
do not do this with jubilation. Give us
the child! Is it a worthy sacrifice? No, but
we must remember. Some have etched
the words into their hearts. So that it
happens again and again. Let us pass.
We are passing.(0,1000)

YEAR (0,1000) -FESTIVAL

F

I

R

?   E

Sirah

Carlos Sirah is a writer and performer from the Mississippi Delta. His work encounters: exile, rupture, displacement, and migration in relation to institutions, local and beyond.

Hyena
an excerpt
Romana Soutus

Tempus Frangit

The audience walks in to see a HY in a cage.

Her hair is wrapped up in pin-curls with bobby pins.

Her face is dewy, but done. Hyper-realistic. Disorienting.

At the top of show she is in white cotton underwear and bra and black heels. Comfortable height. Red bottoms.

She will put on a white wrap dress. Think christening dress made for a child but worn by a teenager. The wrong kind of short. Without the safety pin, it is a touch too low-cut.

Props & Setting

DOG CAGE: It must look rigid in structure, almost rusting. It must be strong enough to support weight. It must also be easy to iron on.

Inside the cage there is a crystal vase, a small bouquet of daisies (no more than 5 but at least 3), iron, hanger, rotisserie chicken, candies/chocolate, an array of fruits including strawberries and watermelon, a platter for said fruit, and a hand-mirror.

The key to unlock the cage will be sitting on top of the cage. It will be almost frighteningly obvious it's sitting there. The light hits it just right that it shines.

Hy is...

Hy is specimen. Hy is prey and predator. Hy does not understand the concept of personal space. Hy simultaneously enjoys and detests being looked at. Hy will eat throughout. Hy does not cry during this show. Ever.

She doesn't know how this will all end.

Embrace the fact that this is in a theatre. Hy certainly will. This is all a
Hy's scene partner is the cage and she struggles with the desire to go
back inside or continue playing out in the world throughout the piece.
She doesn't know how this will end.
Embrace the fact that this is in a theatre. Hy certainly will. This is all a
production, don't try and make it anything else.

HY

Do we all know the story of the little boy who cried wolf?

> (Genuinely asks. She nods, she shakes her head, what
> is it audience???)

I'll tell it to you again... There was once a young shepherd boy who
tended his sheep at the foot of a mountain near a dark forest. It was
rather lonely for him all day, so he made a plan to get a little company
and some excitement. He called out to the village "Wolf! Wolf!" and the
villagers came out to meet him, and some of them stayed with him for a
considerable time. This pleased the boy so much, and the next day he
called out to the village "Wolf! Wolf!", and again the villagers came out
to meet him. On the third day, the Wolf did truly come, and desperately
he called out to the village "Wolf! Wolf!" But this time the villagers, who
had been fooled twice, thought the boy was deceiving them again, and
nobody stirred to come help him. The wolf, having no cause for fear, at his
leisure destroyed the whole flock.

> (Beat.)

What if the boy really did see a wolf every time? What if he wasn't lying?

> (Beat.)

There once was a young shepherdess who tended her sheep at the foot
of a mountain near a dark forest. One hot day, the shepherdess took her
sheep into the forest to get a sip of water from the creek. As the sheep

lapped up the cool creek water, the girl looked in hoping to wash her face. When she looked down into the water she saw a big, scary, wild hyena staring back at her. She shrieked with horror and called out to the village "Hyena! Hyena!". When the villagers came out to meet her they said "there is no hyena". The next day was equally hot, and again the girl took her sheep into the forest to get a sip of water from the creek. As the sheep lapped up the cool creek water, the girl looked in hoping to wash her face. When she looked down into the water she saw a big, scary, wild hyena staring back at her. She shrieked with horror and called out to the village "Hyena! Hyena!". When the villagers came to meet her they said "there is no hyena". On the third day the girl went alone into the forest. The girl looked in the water, and again she saw a big, scary, wild hyena staring back at her. "I'll make them see" she muttered to herself, and the girl, having no cause for fear, at her leisure destroyed the whole flock.

> (Beat. Smile. Hy begins to laugh. A hyena laugh. The laugh peels back her skin to reveal the fur and jutting bones underneath.)

I can just imagine the shepherdess walking into the village. Her pretty dress and delicate hands stained. The villagers stripping her tattered clothes, whispering to her that everything was going to be okay, that they're going to protect her now, caressing her hair, washing her hands for her, making warm stew to settle her upset stomach.

"Goodness, how she must have suffered."/"How brave, how strong"/"What a beautiful girl".

> (Beat.)

I see my beast.

I walk around every day with this beast on a leash.

It wants to rip the chains and run around free and destroy the flock just so people can know its there.

It wants to laugh uproariously, and put honey on its tongue to change its voice, and tear apart a gazelle, and tell people it loves them even though it knows it shouldn't.

This beast looks like me. Like the person you think you know. She has the same curve to her waist and the same giggle.

>(Smile.)

She just has sharper teeth.

>(Beat.)

I just want to talk to you.

I just want to play for a little bit.

I promise I won't bite.

At least not yet.

>(Beat.)

I promise to go right back into this cage when we're done and you won't have to worry about me anymore.

All one of you has to do is come up, pick up that pretty key, and unlock this cage.

>(she points to the key.)
>
>(Sometimes this will be easy. Sometimes this will be hard. Hy has to convince someone in the audience. When the person finally opens the lock, she asks them to wait for a moment. She takes one of the daisies, looks at it, bites the flower off and gives the audience member the stem and a kiss on the cheek. She then lets them return to their seat.)

Romana Soutus is an Ukrainian/Argentinian playwright + performer based in New York City. Her plays include "Hyena" which she performed at La MaMa, the Edinburgh International Fringe Festival and the United Solo festival, and "Martyrs", set to premiere in La MaMa's Spring 2018 season.

20 Feet from Sodom
an excerpt
R. Eric Thomas

Peter and Dwayne's 4th of July Party. Day.

Honey, it's lit. Everyone is standing around the pool in next to nothing. Some of them are actually wearing nothing. Nobody is wearing a shirt. We can't see the pool, just a couple of giant pool floats that bob up and down behind the crowd occasionally. All of the floats are ironic—a seahorse, a pizza, a unicorn, another unicorn, a third unicorn. Everybody bought a unicorn float this year. It's an infinity pool, just so you know. Anyway, you can't see it. You'll never see it. No one is in the pool except Brayden and you'll never see him either, so forget him. Fuck Brayden. (That's another story.)

Who we do see:

Peter and Dwayne in the center, both wearing speedos. They're in their 50s; they've kept it tight, I suppose. White chest hair on deeply tanned chests You know the deal. Peter is white, like Caucasian. Dwayne is mixed race; he'd like you to forget about that, actually. They're leering over a naked white man who is sunbathing on a beach chair between them. This is Perry.

Two other men, Kylie and Deon, standing off to the side. Their bodies are whatever; they're both people of color. Kylie is wearing a jock strap (why?) and Deon is naked but not happy about it.

Beside Kylie and Deon is a Port-a-Potty, which is presently open. A splash from behind the pool floats. They all turn in horror. Freeze. Sound out. Stillness.

In another space: Marilyn. In front of a glass sliding door, half open. She's a regular person but I guess compared to all that, with the dicks and

*the abs and all, she maybe is underwhelming. She's wearing a one-piece
bathing suit and a patterned wrap. Floppy hat. Aunt stuff. She's got three
bracelets: a charm with a bunch of Eiffel Towers, a FitBit and a Life Alert.
(She's allergic to penicillin.)*

*She stares out at us. We are the ocean. She's is on her deck. It slowly becomes
clear that she is next door to Peter and Dwayne. She mutters to herself. We
can't hear her. We can only see her lips move. There's an intensity to her
muttering, as if an incantation. Her eyes pierce the horizon. Marilyn casts an
eye to the party.*

                         MARILYN
What do you think is going on?

              (Beat. She tries again louder.)

What do you think is going on?

              (She turns to look through the door's opening.)

Wonder what's going on.

              (Tanisha pokes her head out of the opening.)

                         TANISHA
Did you hear me?

                         MARILYN
When?

                         TANISHA
Just now.

MARILYN

No. What'd you say?

TANISHA

I said I can't hear you.

MARILYN

Why'd you ask me if I heard that?

TANISHA

Huh?

MARILYN

Why didn't you just assume I couldn't hear you either?

TANISHA

Is that what you were calling in to say? You that invested in my flawed thought process?

MARILYN

No—

TANISHA

I've been sitting at the breakfast table, minding my own black business, watching you chant things at the ocean and casting glances back at me for an hour. I get it. You want my attention.

MARILYN

Why didn't you give me any attention, then?

TANISHA

What do you think this is?

MARILYN

This isn't the attention I wanted.

TANISHA

You get what you get and don't pitch a fit. *(She chuckles.)* Who used to say that?

MARILYN

I don't know.

TANISHA

You get what you get and don't pitch a fit. Who used to say that?

MARILYN

I don't remember.

TANISHA

Okay, well, try to remember? Was is Derek? Was it about per diems? Or paychecks or something?

MARILYN

Derek was never that witty.

TANISHA

It's not that witty; it just rhymes is all. People are beguiled by word sounds.

MARILYN

Well, I don't know who said it.

(Tanisha finally comes out to the deck.)

TANISHA

It'll come to you. *(She looks out over the ocean.)* Waves look good today. *(No response from Marilyn.)* Beach is already crowded. You said it. The 4th of July is always crazy. Look at all those umbrellas. Everybody's so eager to go sit in the sun all day and then not let any sun touch any part of their skin ever.

MARILYN

White people are paradoxical.

TANISHA

There's a black couple over there, looks like. They've got a tent.

MARILYN

Not for long. *(She points.)* Lifeguard already spotted them.

TANISHA

Feel like if they were going to outlaw tents on the beach they should have a sign up or something. That way you didn't go through all the trouble of putting it up just to get told to take it down. *(She chuckles to herself.)* They think they're going camping or something. Or what's the word? Glamping.

MARILYN

You voted for the tent ordinance.

TANISHA

Of course I did. But I didn't vote for there not to be a sign. That just doesn't make any sense. You gotta tell people the rules. That way there's an order to things. Oh. They fought the law and the law won. Down comes the tent. Sorry, brothers.

MARILYN

No kids out there, today. No women either.

TANISHA

Just dicks as far as the eye can see. *(Off Marilyn's look.)* An ocean of dicks.

MARILYN

How you think that happened? Wasn't like that when we bought.

TANISHA

Like attracts like. You show up with your kid and your wife and it's a bunch of fit men in tiny shorts, something probably tells you to keep moving.

MARILYN

When's the last time a straight man ever kept moving from anywhere?

TANISHA

Welcome to the new age. You going out?

MARILYN

Probably. Figured I'd roam the sand like a sea witch, barking at penises and causing general consternation.

TANISHA

Cool. Let me know when you do.

(Tanisha turns to head back in.)

MARILYN

Wonder what's happening over there.

TANISHA

What? You're mumbling. Why are you mumbling?

MARILYN

I said, I wonder what's happening over there?

TANISHA

Peter and Dwayne's? What do you think is happening?

(Tanisha peers over the railing.)

Pool floats. That's new. Floats in the pool but no people.

MARILYN

Nothing wrong with their party.

TANISHA

Never said there was.

MARILYN

Just loud is all.

TANISHA

So early in the day.

MARILYN

Don't mind it.

TANISHA

Just saying.

MARILYN

Sounds like quite a party.

(Beat.)

Wonder what's different.

(Beat.)

Thomas

Can't tell if it's the same men from Memorial Day or—

TANISHA

If you're going to sit here stewing all day—

MARILYN

I'm just wondering. You don't have to listen if it annoys you so much.

TANISHA

Is it bothering you?

MARILYN

No. No. No. No. A little.

TANISHA

You want me to say something?

MARILYN

I can speak for myself.

(Pause.)

TANISHA

I'll go say something.

MARILYN

It's fine. Go back to your black business.

TANISHA

Now I'm distracted. Business is slow.

MARILYN

Looks like a good time.

TANISHA

Marilyn, honestly. Every time with this? Go, don't go, roam the beach barking at dicks. Just do something.

MARILYN

I'm just making conversation.

TANISHA

With who?!

MARILYN

I can't make conversation?

TANISHA

I am barely listening to you. This is not a conversation. This is the inevitable.

MARILYN

I'm not going to go.

TANISHA

Okay.

MARILYN

It's very much not my scene.

TANISHA

Okay.

MARILYN

I'm just saying.

TANISHA

Okay.

MARILYN

I'm busy today.

TANISHA

Sure, honey.

MARILYN

I need to make a sweet potato pie for the function, for instance.

TANISHA

I'm definitely not going to that.

MARILYN

They're expecting you.

TANISHA

They'll have to work through the disappointment.

MARILYN

You said you were coming.

TANISHA

I lied.

MARILYN

You can't lie to church folks.

TANISHA

Actually, you can. More easily, in fact.

MARILYN

Well, I'm going to go.

TANISHA

Do you.

MARILYN

I signed up for the pie.

TANISHA

It wouldn't be the 4th of July without your pie.

MARILYN

It wouldn't.

TANISHA

Have fun.

(Pause.)

MARILYN

I'm going next door first.

TANISHA

I'm shocked.

MARILYN

It's just so loud. I'll say my hellos and then I'll tell them to turn it down.

TANISHA

Okay.

MARILYN

Fifteen minutes, tops.

TANISHA

See you tonight.

MARILYN

Stop. It's not like that.

TANISHA

Just cuz you saved now doesn't mean you can't do body shots with a bunch of naked dudes like the old days.

MARILYN

Actually, it does.

TANISHA

I think you're misunderstanding.

MARILYN

How would you know? You don't even go to church.

TANISHA

I know enough to know the Bible doesn't say "Thou shall not lick, slam and suck off some lithe young thot."

MARILYN

Thot?

TANISHA

It's what they say these days. *(She points over the railing.)* Those are thots.

MARILYN

I don't need that information.

TANISHA

It's yours, free of charge. *(She gives a wave.)* Well, have fun. Mix it up, honey!

MARILYN

I'm just going over to say my hellos.

TANISHA

Whatever hon.

MARILYN

If I'm not back by 2, come get me.

TANISHA

How I'm gonna come get you when I'm already gonna be over there?

MARILYN

You are not!

TANISHA

Those thots aren't going to lick, slam and suck themselves.

MARILYN

I think you're using that wrong.

TANISHA

What part?

MARILYN

All of it?

TANISHA

I guess we'll find out. Lemme get my shoes.

R. Eric Thomas is an award-winning playwright and a Senior Staff Writer at ELLE. com. Find more information at rericthomas.com

POETRY

Diez Formas Para Amar a Tu Suegra (10 Ways to Love Your Mother-in-Law)

Jubi Arriola-Headley

One. Visit her on her birthday. Address the gift card to *Mamá*. Sign it *con un mil abrazos, un mil besos, y amor infinito*, in your best, Googled Spanish. Write the gift card in your handwriting, from both you and her child. Put her child's name first.

Two. Offer to help her prepare dinner. Know that however you knead dough, chop onions, or season the *carnitas* for the *tamales* will be a blasphemy to a chef of her skills. Accept whatever correction she's willing to offer with spoonfuls of grace.

Three. Let her catch you stealing a taste of whatever she's cooking before it's ready, right from the pot. Be unapologetic when she catches you. Say to her, "But it smells so good, *Mamá.*" Fix your lips to pout when she plays at swatting your hand away.

Four. At dinner, let her catch you plucking a piece of lint from her child's shirt, or brushing a rogue hair from her child's cheek.

Five. After dinner, offer to do the dishes. Say "This way you two will have some time to yourselves."

Six. After dishes, offer to drive everyone into town for *helado*. Offer *Mamá* **you**r arm as you escort her to the car. Insist that she ride shot-gun.

Seven. Hold her child's hand as the two of you decide whether to share one or two scoops of pistachio. Or rum raisin.

Eight. Laugh as *Mamá* tells the story of how her child once ran away from home because she refused to serve ice cream for dinner. No matter how many times you've heard this story before.

Nine. When it's time to say goodbye, lean in close, kiss *Mamá* on the cheek, and say to her, "the only thing I love more than your son is your tamales." She will giggle, much like she did back when she wore her hair in pigtails, no matter how many times she's heard this before.

Ten. Melt when *Mamá* touches your hand and says, in her best, Googled English, "I only make my special birthday *tamales* for two people: my son, and the man he married." Melt, no matter how many times you've heard this before.

Bliss?

Jubi Arriola-Headley

Your fingers rip
a river in me, shred skin like
shalestone, flick a nipple into
aftershock, usher up a moan,
a volcanic emission,
spiriting me toward
surrender.

My back, broad as it is,
betrays me – arches, thrusts my
soul toward yours.
Reaching the periphery
of you, I gladly surrender
my sword, my own borders long
since breached, my submission,
infinite.

Is this

Jubi Arriola-Headley is a writer, storyteller, and first-generation American born to Bajan (Barbadian) parents. He's currently working on his first collection of poems. Jubi and his husband divide their time between South Florida and Guatemala, where he hopes to pick up enough Spanish to figure out what his in-laws are saying about him.

When I'm told that chemical disease is some white shit // fast forward 100 years from now.

Kay Ulanday Barrett

the air is a thicket or jar of jam,
people breathe in bulbous catastrophe but with
the layers of plexy glass over faces, *breathing*
    is a loose word.

when you are kissed for the first time, the masks
are off. there is only 3 hours of free space air for us
a day and this is what you choose to do with it:

get wet like the ancestors did before,
fumble hair strands
in eager crooks of palms,
make a garden of the minute,
bury your heart in the mud,
make pulse bigger.

it wasn't always this way.
lovers could sufficiently waste one another's time
on the last planet. this is what the old
media states—
    bumbling lungs that didn't have to beg for air.

now lovers are regimented crash sights.
bodies hover in metal and forget sometimes
that we are something more

than voice boxes in containers.

plants used to be the source,
corals made way for more minutes.
oxygen of earth from earth.

                                        that was then.

on this dome,
you sneak glances over love interests
in aluminum,
save up your devotion
in moments.

now, you can't be remarkable in your eruptions
like your grandparents.
spontaneity is fossil.
fingertips have long forgotten
the concept of kinetic.
what do you do when humanity is a boundary breached?
        why did it get to this point—

lung rigor slice, resentment gut,
god what *would* you do if anyone actually touched
your cheek without planning to?

a new life they promised.
one better after the climate
stopped grappling with mistakes.

and now to kiss is
daydream thing.
love,
        artifact.

people are in cases and
tired of all this accumulation.

you must finds ways.
take off your helmet.
welcome the storm.

let's learn to breathe again
      or let us just cherish this air,
      let us inhale even it breaks us for trying.

the gender spectrum
Kay Ulanday Barrett

"I know what it is to be broken and be bold
Tell you that my silver is gold"
—Moses Sumney

when all your skin / reads // trespass / reads not worth // a piss /
literally / not / worth excrement / reads good // enough to not be
dead // maybe if she sleeps with me / i am trained to think / pity

once / a man spat in my face // kicked / my cane / touched his
dick like a small itch / i erased / into words like // dyke she-man die die /
you're never going to be / real // he says

as i was saying // another dude pushed me / stalked // me for blocks until
i turned the corner / and faked a call // on my / cell phone
that guy said / you don't have any friends // and he wasn't wrong exactly

i am not a real man / i'm beyond // this doesn't happen to / everybody
right to be real // doesn't mean a war to meet someone's / parents or / be
able to wear a shirt at the mall // because what is your love / but shame /
worthy

this world / makes me feel that way // no matter the / constellation
of well intentioned quotes / or rainbow like buttons // or safety pins /
i am pinned down / everywhere / i go // no words can be barrier /
for night terrors / so i make // like a flicker / smile at parties / which is a
lie really

for wanting / to be here // which is the scapegoat / of something

larger // says my therapist / and he quotes me throwing fire / back
to my heart / when all I want is to be melted // not almost ashes /

another dark poem / says another editor // and I think
this is nothing / I have a therapist at least // picture an alley / where
your legs are tangled to / dumpster groans // and if actually / reported on

the news / they jam / you between / a funny bird story / and a partly
sunny forecast / and for fifteen seconds / the anchor / doesn't blink and
bet you // they get / your name wrong / again // hashtag here.

Tibo: Akong Kasaysayan
After Gloria Anzaldúa
Kay Ulanday Barrett

A child isn't so much a discovery
but a dragging.

Forward

    Rene Fornnes is informed that I am
    in love with her.

    Joseph Pinkett found a love letter
    I wrote and stole it, gave it to her.

    She kisses me in the basement
    after CCD class for approximately
    six minutes
    six lifetimes
    six laps in kilometers

    or miles
    or basically,
    my mouth feels like galaxy.

    My thumbs
    become bruises after signing
    the cross so many times.
    Fair exchange.

Forward
>Still refuse anything
>but shorts and pants.

>I scrape my knees from a
>belly kick
>telling me,
>>be a girl
>>be a girl.

Forward
I crave that 1.5 inch gap between the skirt
and whatever happens between inner thighs.

>The.   gap.

>Sylvia was the first girl to take me there,
>where I stayed.
>I never wanted to leave.

Forward
//// Kicked out
//// Spat at
//// *You are not my child!*

Found me making out with my first real girlfriend.
Here, learn kissing can be mistaken for bloodletting.

My mama turned anything that belonged to me &
made it weapon.

Whole hopes thrashed to dust.

My heart,
there,
a crater.

Forward
Reconciliation is
a mother who
refuses to look you in the eye.

In response,
I move the food to the tenor of small talk
I am terrible at.

Forward
     Only talk about meals
     how the crab was,
     did the fish need more salt?
     Treaties signed by taste buds.

     I plan vacation the same time
     mama goes back home sa Pilipinas.
     Remember: during our final goodbye
     (I didn't know that then),
     she swells up in my hands.

     It's as though all of her becomes blanket or dough.
     After this, I never see her again.

The next time she
    arrives to greet you,
    accept the ashes.

Kay Ulanday Barrett aka @brownroundboi, has featured globally; Princeton University, UC Berkeley, The Lincoln Center, Queens Museum, The Chicago Historical Society, The Guild Complex, to name a few. Contributions include: PBS News Hour, The Margins, RaceForward, Foglifter, The Deaf Poets Society, Poor Magazine, Fusion.net, Trans Bodies/Trans Selves, Winter Tangerine, Make/Shift, Buzzfeed, The Huffington Post, The Advocate, and Bitch Magazine. kaybarrett.net

Centralia

Sara Bess

The coal mine beneath Centralia, Pennsylvania has been burning since 1962. Everyone has long since fled, but I'm still haunting the ghost town. On occasion, I conjure a cool breeze to rattle a few loose window panes. I've thought about hiring an exorcist, but who would pay the bill?

Springfield

(first published in Plenitude)
Sara Bess

I am the only one here
with all my fingers.

My boss is impressed by this
and by the fact that I have never
shot myself

with a nail gun, though I am afraid
of the loud noises of the air compressor
of the dust and the splinters. I am careful
with my hands.

By Friday my mucus is dark
with blood and sawdust and I
am coughing worse than usual,
but I am very precise. My careful hands—

with all their fingers
all their ragged ends—are good
in small spaces. I have lived
my whole life in spaces like these.

Sara Bess grew up in rural southeast Missouri but she doesn't live there anymore. Her work has appeared in The Wanderer, Witch Craft Magazine, and elsewhere.

Bess

Let It

Rachel Brownson

Oh, love, sometimes
the animal tries to escape
your shuttered chest.

Today, again, blood.
Just blood again, out
where it shouldn't be,
cooling around each wound,
and it goes
everywhere, gloveprints
on bleached towels, foot smudges
on polished floors—
                                    The way
a baby's head just fits
into your hand like that. Hot
on the palm, the hot curve
of the head, silky damp curls.
I've held a lot of them,
some of them dead,
none of them mine.
Like that. Things do settle.

Mare Anguis
Serpent Sea
Rachel Brownson

I drowned   those nights.
Seaweed rippled   in my torso's

warming sea,   snarled
in pleural crevices,   crept

up my throat's   silted channel.
Eels sidled narrow bodies   along

passages that once   swelled   with air
(when my body was a body still),

snapped   their jaws   when sleep
threatened   to carry me off

on its slow tide.   And each wave
was an hour,   and each hour

washed over me,   as my sister
slept   curled on the shore

of the other bed,   moonlight trickling
across her back,   her long braid

snaking down the mattress edge.

A Prayer

Rachel Brownson

Today it is the God
in the bread, the texture
nothing like flesh
except in the kneading,
beaten until it springs
back soft as a breast.

God in the bread, today
this flesh springs back
still soft as the day
I learned that to slap
these thick thighs red
was to know myself
righteous, to know
this wrong body
checked: if it couldn't
be loved it could be
punished. God

in the bread, what flesh
is permissible? what death
do you ask of flesh?

*Rachel Brownson is a writer and hospital chaplain in Ann Arbor, MI, and holds
an MFA in creative writing from Warren Wilson College.*

On First Meeting my Future Husband-Wife (Or, when the Aquarians Declare Affection)

Kayleb Rae Candrilli

In 48 hours I say hello and goodbye so many times my tongue rolls like hard candies spilled from a blue glass bowl. One day soon I will give you a ring made exclusively of my white hairs. There are ways to make knots new: something home grown, stratus clouds, a prayer and a mantis walking—stilt legs stippling the water. When we boil ourselves down to the base, gravity is heavy love and every poem is really a poem about aging, counting seconds as stars, or as skips of a rock along what mirages silken. We were born under the same sun sign, and can I ask you what hemisphere looks up our skirts on the first day of spring? Can I ask if this where we keep secrets for one another? Little water bearers. What if we spill and break all this celestial balance?

When I learn you, I learn everything has to be blue and yellow and bloodied with wine rivering from a box. If I learn myself, malt is the way my lips taste and you like it that way—raw sugar, fermentation, something that's been around just a little too long. You tell me you'd like to visit the Grand Canyon, but first, what about somewhere underwater? Let's become amphibious; let's gill ourselves like wishing well pennies; let's drink the fountain of youth. If the world reminds us that you're the young one, may I drink from you? And since you're the young one, I promise to keep you so: my hair as your pearls—iridescent; everything about you: new and wet and shining.

A Night on the Town with My Future Husband-Wife

Kayleb Rae Candrilli

They steal shot glasses, carry a fleet of tiny drinks in their bag and whisper to me the importance of hydration. They plan to steal palm trees, too. Rip them from the roots and keep the bulbs in their pockets as neon light. I tell them, I'll learn to drive if they'll let me be the getaway. Which they understand as me admitting love and all the ways I am willing to make my body move for them. They use their hands to say things like: let's make coffee, let's go out dancing, let's swim through coral and trapeze through what's on fire. They sign and I transliterate: let us lake in cotton sheet, get low & loud fence sing, leg & fin the rough corral—end & trap ease threw want & desire. I say, *for you I'd light the world on fire.* So they pull me inside and say *it's already burning.* The sky licks red cumulous along our thighs. They ask, *what's the third degree if not a way to learn?*

Kayleb Rae Candrilli is author of What Runs Over with YesYes Books and winner of the 2016 Pamet River Prize. They are published or forthcoming in BOAAT Press, Puerto del Sol, Booth, Vinyl, Muzzle, Cream City Review, and others.

pygmalion_s_bad_bxtch.gif
jayy dodd

i've been [un]making myself. what's good [?] - boy
carving bad-womxn out of his own data. extract
his pxssy from the download. drag all the junk to
the trash.   empty. empty. e v e r y w e e k .
every 30 days. automatically. empty. there is never
enough space to save. i've been needing an
upgrade. it feels like every week i crash. a restart is
required. *would you like to restart now? tonight? in one*
hour? in one week? you have to close all windows.
save your work. i learned this the hard way: my
software is not compatible, yet i can reformat files
from previous editions of myself. how i have only
so much memory. i try to store myself externally.
FILE TOO BIG. NOT ENOUGH SPACE. my
desires fit into 500x500px. my adoration goes
viral. how many fingers can react, before i am real?
i program my own weird science, to transmit the
body   I   have   yet   to   see   embed.

death_by_dxks.mp3
jayy dodd

a tombstone
peaks from under my skirt.
above a 7-inch satin-lined casket.

when you touch it
we're both mourning.

the illusion i am living, is life.

hide the rotting with perfume & daffodils.
a cemetery is always a garden.

return for the exposed root.
life protrudes from seemingly lifeless earth.
my roots exposed grave & tragic to the living.

here, the wake is the risk.
memorial can only be celebration.
we have parades for a reason. dying
out in the streets must call for some anthem.

Fuck It (We Have Right Now!)

the belting chorus-line of sisters trails
down the river, cross the feed, into the night.

we carry out urns tucked underneath
— our throats

self.jpg
jayy dodd

a spectral moment   extension
in all directions a trajectory of failure
      function: kind/ of woman/
hint   clue   acrylic keystroke
a knowing signal   kindness
is a shared language   a sweet word
a look   *function:* [in]visible/ [un]seen
a recognition of subtly   a transaction of
bijou pleasantries.   a gilded smudge
a wet sable accent purring in the corner
a mouth   a mouth adorned
held tight until a luster breaks forth
a clicking   a humming   suckling
of air behind clenched teeth
      function: compress/ all possibleselves
[re]format   delete create
a new *function:* indicate/ living
processing the most

jayy dodd is an blxk trans femme writer & artist. they talk shit on the internet & their words are award-nominated & generally controversial.

Molluscs

Kenan Ince

In my fantasies I'm always walking
downstairs in my sensible flats.
Something about them arouses me:
the way they can be so easily slipped
off, their black skeletons crumpling
in my closet until I am ready to give
them flesh. They are no animal.
They are as little as possible
between me and the caress
of the earth on my feet. Oh,
how Donald Trump would love
for me to take them off
and float through the halls
behind him like a caveman's
wife, hand on my swollen belly!
How Donald's mouth would swell
on the aerodynamic curved tip
as I inserted my foot, softly,
between his lips. How
he would suck as if to aspirate
out the vital part of me.
And how he would gasp, his lungs
collapsing into the garden
of his ribs, his words scurrying
before they are spoken
from the shell of his mouth.

Snowglobe

Kenan Ince

My cyborg-smooth silver face
drained of pressure, collapsing onto
eroded cheekbones. Under my skin,
cell after cell containing copies
of Grandpa's closet of starched
white shirts, American flag patches
sewn onto short sleeves. I used
to make myself small, curl into a ball
with flashlight and yellowed,
smoke-drenched library book, my
face caressed by adjacent shirttails.
In the book's hard-backed walls
slept incantations for conjuring
worlds. Always more room
in small things—my whirring
mitochondria holding copies
of Grandma's chest of doll parts,
which I glued together, heads
to torsos, a benevolent creator god.
Inside that room the glittering
forest of my queerness sprouted.
My DNA: stacked replicas of the
old house's impossibly twisted
staircase, miraculously held
together by wooden pegs, bounded
four feet above by wooden ceiling,
under which I squatted with Game
Boy for hours. After running
downstairs, I'd pause to stare
at the globe where a troupe
of porcelain ballerinas twirled
to soundless music, a murmuration
of flakes around them—
globes within globes. I'd like to
throw open the windows of my
body, let in the ion breeze, but
sometimes the walls are all that
keep in the many-mirrored snow.

Kenan Ince is a mathematician, poet, and organizer from Denton, TX, living on occupied Shoshone, Paiute, Goshute and Ute territory (so-called Salt Lake City). Their work is forthcoming in Pleiades and Duende and has appeared in Word Riot and Permafrost, among others.

Half-truth
(after Frank Bidart)
Omotara James

for N.L.

That suburban Saturday morning we
did handstands in my mother's pool, legs agape

and unbothered in our round browns—no one
to point out our similar otherness, as if the pigments

of our lives weren't a constellation of charted
compliments, through Oprah Major and Whoopi's Minor

limbs, outstretched in a porcelain tub of milk. We dunked
each other's heads into that summer of chlorine

until we came up wholesome, again, for the first time.
Sisters. We were usually mistaken

while standing in line for the movies, by a couple
of older boys, often men,

our adjacent limbs and torsos reflecting
the other's parallel ebbs and flows

—nobody knows about that morning,
the look on my face.

Natasha, last month I saw you
for the first time in years

you were always only
a late night Google of words

away. The text beneath your name,
an expiration date

just shy of a year. Sour
that you can't absolve me

of the horror on my face:
the shape of rejection still opens my lips.

Only sister I ever loved, we
won't have the conversation

now, that ends with *yes,*
I knew. That begins:

Natasha, I am sorry,
for avoiding water all these years,

for leaving you to tread.
I had hoped our conversation would end

on either one's front porch, two old
loud & cackling bitches, smug & thin

with forgetting what the world
should have already known.

James

Carryin' on
like before they killed Michael

like before they hipped Lionel, singing
say you, say me, say always…

like before I said *I love you,*
but not that way.

Abecedarian for Leaving

Omotara James

Anatomy	was never my passion,
beneath	the fat
continues	a cruelty time
divides as	a banana peels:

everyday,	in silence
forgotten,	alongside the
greater	
higher	power.

I squat beneath heaven, for some
juxtaposition.

Knowing
love
means
nothing

occurs without
penance. I didn't open the
Qur'an you threw at me, for weeks. Now it
reads like
songs we sing against our bodies,

the pages torn
up with
violence. I pray

we ripen before we learn the word for fruit, your
x tried to tell me

you'd never un-
zip the cruelty.

Omotara James writes and lives in New York City. She is an MFA candidate at NYU. Her poetry chapbook, Daughter Tongue, is forthcoming from APBF and Akashic Books. Her debut full length collection, Mama Wata is forthcoming from CCM press. For inquiries, visit www.omotarajames.com

concrete can't help/ but betray itself in smoothness

Hannah Rubin

Midnight sees distinctive flutters in the redness of the CVS sign. I hold
your cup close to chest so my fingertips can touch.

Milk is thick when you drink it slowly.
Night is warm when it touches skin.

Or maybe I've gotten that wrong — and skin is warm
when it touches night. I'm here but the buildings have no edges,

a periphera of dust slipping and shedding. On the corner, by the In
N' Out, there is a tall carton of hamburger buns stacked in twelves.

I can't help but notice — feel wracked by —
how I lean into you

when I'm okay, I lean out of you when I'm not. But I digress.
When the twelve lane highway becomes thirteen, the preoccupied

mother frequently intrudes. I take my shoes off because I want to queer
this place. *CARS* blinks in rainbow: I am barely alone.

Come to my house and dance neon with me. Surely, I will already be
asleep. Surviving it: not one, they say, but two of us.

untitled mourning
Hannah Rubin

— black dress & ginger threaded beard

breaking na'an while a woman outside
screams *hunger*

never loved out my body
to another body (never let myself
do full loving)

Hannah Rubin

loved so full in my body screamed
cried tore in my body hell-on-earth
to my body bottled up and
crawling ears to floor, to wall, to
surface. I was of my body and
I was out of my body but never
to another body through exchange
of a promise, a promise saying
here I am I hear you.

Hannah Rubin is a poet and visual artist living in Los Angeles, CA. They are the founder of Poetry in the Dark, a communal sound experiment, and a co-curator for The Poiesis Project, a series of curated political posters, in collaboration with writer Tara Marsden and BAMPFA. You can find recent art & writing in Entropy Magazine, HOLD: A Journal, and Heavy Feather Review.

In Which Heartbreak
Natalie A. Sharp

I became a mother
with my fingers

still wet with daughtering.
I lived in a stone

ship on the shoreline and believed
I could learn

to swim simply by breathing
a sea of water in—

When the stone spat
back, I looked down and held

a child.
You embarked on a surgery

to separate, finally
from the center

of your pain. I feel
the aching through the hole

closed up like an empty piercing.
I think it was the cancer

of your runaway child,
The old incisive habit

to cut away
before my face begins

to round into your same
curves, a hint of your dimple

in my right
cheek, I am so much

you

Daughter Like Murder
Natalie A. Sharp

I have been dead for four years.
I ghost through the walls of my childhood
home, watching my photographer mother
finger fading images of me.

I am in the whisper-thin pages of the Bible
she oils with her palms, trying to
forget me—
I cautionary tale I gay shame I locked closet red

dress dead daughter.
I do not know where my body is buried.
It is so strange to know no plot
bears your name, no stone annotation to summarize
this queer life.

I find my phantom face
salty and confused contorted
mask of suffering.
This disownership is an immolation
by degrees, the crimson ferocity of it

meant to bring me back
to the god I don't put in my poems
because my life is
none of that vindictive motherfucker's business.

My tongue glows like poker my

body becomes whip either way I lick
lacerate sky why do your own
daughter like murder, like arson
come to creep slow burn
your paradise to ash?

I shatter I nowhere girl I candlelight
in vacuum I know night I translucent
torso I ghost pen ghost writer no hands I

fancy footwork
limp breath
split sternum
metaphor
cut short

the mother's pantoum//1
Natalie A. Sharp

You've never even asked me about flight.
The night after your father died,
I lay awake remembering
stars threatening to swallow us whole.

The night after your father died,
seared breath of the Earth. Half my works:
stars threatening to swallow us whole
and now they have. But I survived.

Seared breath of the Earth: half my works
lie in making sense of the senseless,
and now they have. But I survived
long enough to wish a daughter on the sky.

I can't wait until you have a teenaged child.
I lay awake remembering
You cry, *maybe you'll understand why I left.*
You've never even asked me about flight.

Natalie A. Sharp is a Black queer writer, dancer, and activist based in Denver, CO. A 2016 Pushcart Prize nominee, Natalie is currently pursuing an MFA in Creative Writing with a concentration in poetry at the University of Colorado at Boulder, where she also teaches undergraduate creative writing.

Saving Lives
Jane Starr

Here's proof parents sane enough to stand trial let me chill with their
first born no matter what the stupid law says. My friend Ken is a computer tech. His wife is a librarian. They're dorks. But they have a daughter
named Abby. She's thirteen she's cooler than all of us I've never been
more pissed. I knew it the moment I saw her. It's just one of those things.

I hate five out of four teenagers. From thirteen to nineteen kids are extra
useless. I have zero compassion for their awkward developing little lives.
Nothing makes my skin crawl like the sound of young people enjoying
themselves. Have you ever heard one talk. Gross. I dont care about fucking a hot eighteen year old. I care about burying one with a shovel after
a dirtbike race. That's my teen fantasy. What the fuck is wrong with you.

I only like teenagers that are one in a million. I only like teenagers that
are mere steps away from becoming the coolest person ever. I've seen
this happen twice and no I'm not one of them you smart aleck cocksuck-
ers.

When I was a teenager all of the adults deserved to die by ripping heli-
copter blades. Pretending like they had their shit together while doling
out shame. Godless. It wasn't just the abuse of power, it was being forced
to witness such a tawdry paper thin charade.

Don't think I Don't Know you're one step away from another broken
relationship/filing for bankruptcy/"hanging yourself" like that guy from
inxs. The only reason you're trying to teach me a lesson is because your
life is shambles you damage. Get in your car and kill yourself.

I only liked adults that gave me money. I only liked adults so hardened madonna hot I wanted them to replace my parents. Much like today.

The only adult I ever listened to was ray liotta that one time he convinced me to not join the mafia. And that was only because he was so charismatic so good looking so able to say shit in just the right way.

"If you're part of a crew nobody ever tells you that theyre going to kill you. It doesnt happen that way. There arent any arguments or curses like in the movies. Your murderers come with smiles. They come as your friends. The people who've cared for you all of your life. And they always seem to come at a time that you're at your weakest and most in need of their help."

I have zero ties to the mafia to this day.

Since abby was thirteen I privately threaten her parents into letting her watch fight club immediately. Listen you fucks I whisper, looking them both dead in their dumb parent eyes-

You make Me sick. You really think I wouldnt notice the lack of darkness in that girl's face, how obvious it is she's never seen a real movie before. That kid's gonna be in high school soon you sadist fucks-why dont you just buy a baby deer and smash it through a thirteenth floor plate glass window instead.

She needs to know that it's only after we've lost everything that we're free to do anything. That our great war is a spiritual war. That our great depression is our lives.

Look when I was thirteen my dad made me watch wild at heart/taxi driver/every epidode of twin peaks plus fire walk with me and I turned

out absolutely fucking flawless. Then I make that sweeping motion with
one delicate alabaster hand down my to die for figure. Grow the fuck up
I snarl, my teeth gritted. Just do it fucking do it do it—Thank you. Jesus.

I take abby to a convenient store to get fight club snacks. Since she
deserves to live and I'm the only radical beautiful adult she'll ever meet,
I tell her the two things I wish someone had said that one right way to me
so I would've actually listened as we walk.

Kid im sorry about your parents— you're just gonna have to do your
best. She nods quietly. Okay cool.

The day is a pale and looming grey. There's a valero two blocks up. I
couldn't remember the last time I had walked this far. I grab her shoulder, scaring the living shit out of her— Look at me okay. Just fucking look
at me. This is gonna start out so hecka epically lame. But it gets better so
just deal. Understand.

She stares into my burning yellow eyes with her way too innocent
ones(christ this kid needs to see a fucked up movie like now—) and says
yeah. Okay. (oh fuck she's so calm what a boss) Supercool. Walk.

I talk quickly cause I hate it when anyone older says shit all slow for emphasis. It makes me want to break their jaw with my elbow for emphasis
all smash smash smash smash ohhhh how's that for emph—

Here's the deal—

Fuck everyone. There's only one dumb thing you can do that will fuck
you forever—smoke cigarettes. I don't care if you shoot heroin with aids
glazed needles. Go join a cult and get devirginized by their leader and
start cranking out babies and murdering them with a meat cleaver. Tonight. You've got a better chance of surviving those things by far.

Now I know you have idiot mallslut girlfriends that smoke marlboro vanilla lights on the reg. Did they already pull you in with their little witch
claws or not. Dont fuck me. Dont lie. I'm not gonna tell your parents. I
dont give a fuck about your parents. They're on their way out.

No she finally says. They've asked me to but I haven't yet.

Holyfuckingshit I whisper scream. When I was your age I was on my way
to smoking crack out of coke cans with a vengeance. Okay. Those little
hookers in training—they're not your friends. They're weak. They're shit.
They cant help you. Drop them. Trade up. They're gonna become worn
down nags at forty that should get shotgunned behind a barn somewhere.

That's the deal. That's what nobody understands going in. No one gets
out. No one quits. Ever. Now do any of these teenskeezes have moms that
smoke. Yeah this one girl does— And she looks tore the fuck up doesnt
she, like a scarecrow with highlights that got slow roasted in a tanning
bed right. I watch her face pale with this reckoning. Her head goes up
and down gravely as we enter the valero.

Get whatever the fuck you want I tell her. Just keep listening.

Have you noticed the faint little stitch like lines around this sea horse's
juvedermed lips I ask as we grab sour patch kids and reeses and skors
and gummibears. I bet her eye sockets look like they're always recov-
ering from a bare knuckle boxing match— Omg she totally does abby
whispers, jayden says she wants a facelift for christmas— Youre fucking
A she wants a facelift for christmas. Do you know what that count skanku-
la wants for valentine's day— A New Life.

Abby starts snickering. I know I tell her. It's really funny oh shit oh shit. Now how old is this pirate husk I ask, grabbing a coke zero. She's like forty. Disgusting. I'm thirty six. Omg. You're goddamned right. Part of it's my sailor mouth and twelve year old demeanor but most of it's my creamy smooth milky complexion. Cmon let's buy this shit. What's up bbgrl I tell the lady behind the counter, slamming down a bill. Abby's trying to hand me money saying but my dad gave it to me— Keep the money. Just say you spent it. It's not lying I promise I tell her grabbing the candy.

As we're walking back I hurry things along—

I smoked two packs a day from thirteen to twenty. I wanted to look cool. I didnt think I was enough. There's never another other reason. Then I watched fight club. Over and over at the theater like a lunatic. It clicked. I was buying my own slow shit death.

Everyone would get rich off my corpse. From the tobacco companies to the hospitals to the funeral parlors. I dont want an expensive death. I'd rather get torn apart in a wheat thresher or murdered in mexico for my organs or slowly strangled to death by a psycho ex girlfriend. At least there's honour there. Quitting was impossible. I havent had a drag in six-teen years. I'd rather suck a .45 to the hilt. So don't fuck yourself. Got it. She nods. Or I'll come back here and kill you myself with jumper cables. Got it. She nods again.

I hate kids. You're awful. You're so dumb. I hate you. I hate you even more because you're not I tell her. But it's a good hate. Now give me a hug you little bastard. Aunt jane loves you. If anyone at school start giving you shit you call me. You will never see them again.

We watch fight club. She turns to me after. Vulpine. Predatory. Beautiful. I want to watch it again she says. No fucking shit I tell her.

I can't stop smiling. On the way out I give her twenty bucks. Shut the fuck up and take the money. Buy some mascara. Eyeliner. Lip gloss. Less is more. You'll stand out from your slutbag "friends" even more. Most boys are tools. Make them buy you shit.

Dominatrix. Prost. Film. Skate. Fuck.
Instagram-@missjanestarr
That's more than enough about jane.

Preta

Karina Vahitova

behind the armory in the night a woman with a gurney
pulls the past forth to the water

in the mornings dives one hundred meters into the italian sea
pulls the loose hairs from the rare mouths
of girls, weaves her grandmother's memory
by the shore's edge at dawn.

*

inside my gut pulses my Mother's broken wrist
when i awake cold at twilight
in a quarry among fossils made in ice.

"k béregu," she says
and i pull them towards the pier
one   by one ——
each like a useless curtain.

though i see abject horror, i receive disparate stillness :
above water :
behind me :
my harvest :
shattered corpora :

body of glass
rose against ice.

*

where is it now —
the body obliged in prayer
allegiant heavy to a bludgeon.

i search in letters often, sometimes in numbers
i learn when a 3 marries its shadow in a mirror
it carries 8 lives unseen.

what is impossible graduates to reality by dropping three octaves.

*

timelessness gnaws at elegy —
how many women die with their mouths open?
come back as poltergeist
floating antiphonal

& elysian

with terrible treasures still inside them.

*

silver deer painted by moonlight
fight against their own light
disappear in the elms

and i hear Oldness
Something quickerdying
ricochet of the pulse
singing her locks into

a wind clad in silk.

*

what i see and what i hear
delineates the mythologies i've been tasked with

i search
in the brilliance,
and the veracity of what they could not say
wraps around my basic spine :

the woman hidden in the pulpit —
has she lied down there my whole life
so that i'd learn that
when i kneel

i kneel
on her

only in lucid memory am i rhetorical
autodidact at the hand of antinome grace :

i dignify
i promise
but never enough times

i must learn
to take the water
out of our
mouths.

Much Of Survival On Fire
After Adrienne Rich's essay Compulsory Heterosexuality
and Lesbian Existence
Karina Vahitova

i was dragging our post-Soviet cell,
a bloodline becoming itself at my bloody ankle
only as something i dragged forward
to where the oikos kept its walls,
to where we brought our love and they gave us bricks,
to where all the glass windows never recovered.
what do we owe to each other now when the worst has surpassed us vitally
and who threw out my whole body onto the street?
the man inside your mouth —
i was picking up the silks of you on my way out of the house,
clutching them to my lips.
faces make words erupt
       and mother perhaps i was always building you a mantel
       and more, perhaps change was always coming.
       i never married after you were gone,
       your disavowal is a veil fallen on the back of the dress.
       i have been becoming something you've been.
before i see a will to change, i will have seen much of survival on fire.

Karina Vahitova is a post-Soviet queer poet and movement artist from Kiev, Ukraine living in New York. She has previously worked with Opportunity Project helping to develop healing art therapy programs for individuals with brain damage. She led and managed the global research and performance art archive project at Marina Abramovic Institute. Currently, she volunteers as a rape and domestic violence crisis counselor with Crime Victims Treatment Center. She is a co-founder of The Void Academy and is working on her first book of lyrical theory about female queerness, totalitarianism, violence, and women in the Soviet Union. karinavahitova.com

WRITERS IN RESIDENCE

Fire Hazard
Nahshon D. Anderson

The moon peeked as the sun rose embracing my weary soul. In the midst of yawning and lifting my hands up to the heavens, I gazed oranges, pinks, yellows, and reds, a fire in the sky. The birds' morning ritual of singing and chirping My cue to hit it to Jack-in-the-Box for a supreme croissant combo. This greasy bacon and ham with sunny side up egg in a croissant with hash browns, reminded me of my childhood. But something was whispering in my ear, "Girl just stay out a lil bit longer maybe you'll get lucky!"

One time in my life I had a promise of a better tomorrow, but not the fall of 2006. I was bored out of my mind and battling insomnia, up to old my old shenanigans, failing to wean myself off a nasty addiction to gutters, sidewalks, mooning and accepting rides from strangers. I was in major denial. I desired love but didn't know how to go about receiving it. A decade earlier, due to extreme predation, my trust in humans had been shattered. It didn't help that over the years I only heard of a few stories regarding men of color and transgenders who had lovers. The shame heaped upon us prevented genuine healthy relationships from flourishing. And there was a barrage of messages that we don't deserve much, cemented in my psyche. I felt unworthy of love and respect, so I sealed my heart off and settled for anonymous sex.

I then discovered I could make money using my feminine wiles instead of giving it away which led me to becoming a prostitute. This is a partial narrative of a demoralizing part of my life and how sashaying up and down the streets until the wee hours of the morning to earn discretionary income and affection changed my outlook on relationships and love and how the streets of Hollywood paid off for me in multiple ways.

It was extremely unusual for me to linger in the streets past sun up. When the stars were shining and men were on the hunt it was all good, but when the lights were on turning tricks I lowered my head in disgust and didn't want to be associated with my main hobby. I wasn't ready to retire and get some shut eye, so I hung around, standing near Santa Monica and Highland north of the Public Storage. I stood at the corner next to Shakey's Pizza hoping Eddie would come and rescue me the way he did Shalmor in May of 1997 or better yet, how Hugh, gave Divine a ride.

A black Ford Expedition with tinted windows had sped around the corner numerous times and eventually pulled up curbside. I became hesitant as usual, but once the windows rolled down and I got a good glimpse of the driver, the butterflies began tap dancing in my stomach. He had kinky hair, big lips and hands, thick thighs, with a complexion as deep as dark chestnut and well groomed. I knew he was my ride home.

"Hey girl, what's up? You got a nice ass there. I see you like showing it off."

Licking my lips, I replied, "I'd love to show you more if you let me in."

Unlocking the doors, he whispered "I'm Andre, I don't have that much."

With that invite, I introduced myself as Kina and flew in the car quicker than Serena Williams hitting a tennis ball. I'd become accustomed to flying into cars because standing on the corner bent over negotiating for too long meant risking arrest. Andre could've easily been an NBA player, a jock weighing about 240 lbs. and solid. On the rear of his truck was a small sticker that said *Los Angeles Fire Department*, so I knew he was just the one to extinguish my fire.

Due to my photographic memory, I always noticed and remembered very minute details that anyone else would have just glanced over. As we drove off into the sunrise, I was thrilled that I wasn't one of the other remaining prostitutes that had to suffer during daylight as their makeup ran and their five o'clock shadows surfaced when they struggled on the corner trying to earn money for their cigarettes, hits of crack, crystal aka Tina, black market hormones and back room silicone injections, malt liquor, piss and cum stained, bed bug and cockroach-infested weekly motel rooms. I never had that problem because I had undergone years of laser hair removal, costing me thousands of dollars. Andre handed me two Andrew Jacksons. I directed him to an area on Willoughby and Highland that I was familiar with, onward to the Gilmore gas station built in 1935, which had been closed for years.

Five years prior, in December 2001 when I made my debut on Santa Monica Boulevard, I was waiting for customers in front of Circus Circus, a Gay club that had predominantly Latin clientele. A white truck cruised by. The driver was in his mid-30s, a white guy. I hopped in. I directed him to the Gilmore gas station. Once parked he asked what radio station I wanted to listen to, which was odd. He then he asked me to retrieve his wallet from under the seat. I slightly put my left arm down to access his wallet and heard a thump in the back. *Hmm ok,* I just thought for a second *must be a dog or another type of small animal.*

Then a pale pig shouted, "You're under arrest. Put your hands behind your back!"

For a moment, I thought they may have been serial killers who were attempting to kidnap me. My fears were doused when they transported me to LAPD Hollywood Division without any injuries, where I was booked for solicitation. I was released with a summons to appear in court for the first of my many arrests.

Back to me and Andre, we sneaked into some bushes, he bent me over, grunted and after thrusting for three minutes, we were both glowing full of glee, wiping our hands on our pants as we scurried back inside his vehicle. He then dropped me off near my home. Days later, I was back to my usual illicit parade of tricks. It was a routine that I could perform in my sleep, which brought me great satisfaction and cheap thrills. I would quickly bend over, acting like a bar of slippery soap had fallen out of my hands and my long t-shirt would rise up to reveal my tights with a large hole cut out around the ass cheek part. The musician Prince was my inspiration for the pants he wore back in the late 80s. On a ton of occasions, I would purposely expose my anus to make sure I grabbed the drivers' attention to ensure I had a customer.

Guys would honk their horns, some would ride by with taunts, shouting *you nasty ass faggot, how big is your dick, you're going to hell, he bitch, fudge packer,* of course, the most popular, which I *loved* to hear, was *how much?* I would also have to duck for cover dodging their unmerciful hurling of eggs, bottles, bricks, bullets, bats, cups of shit and piss, chains, and white LAPD officers riding around with their pants halfway down playing with their lil two-inch friends. One evening I attracted the attention of a car full of young black males. They became overly excited in their attempt to get closer to me and a few exited the vehicle. I then contemplated if I was going to have to scale a fence and felt like I was escaping from Alcatraz to get out of their car's way to avoid meeting their bender and the pavement.

I wreaked a ton of havoc while in the streets due to my subconscious desire for self-destruction. The adrenalin rush I received while acting like prey from the vultures was beyond satisfying the excitement staved off my boredom, kept me from crying and let me with an endless supply of stories. Thanks to Prince, I made a ton of money but made the other prostitutes gnash their teeth and want to bury me.

Back at work, Andre the firefighter scooped me up. I was dying to strip him and this time, I said, "let's go to my house so we could be more comfortable." I lived five minutes away. We arrived at my house and, upon entering, fireworks briefly erupted and sizzled out. We then exchanged phone numbers. On more than one occasion while peering out my window I would see him zip by. I couldn't understand why he was making me the focus of his attention, patrolling my street without phoning me and offering assistance. I asked myself during the next few weeks. *Will Andre's benevolence erupt into malevolence?* Was he hiding ulterior motives as other men did?

So many men up until meeting Andre had broken me. Experience had taught me that momentary kind-heartedness was not to be believed because eventually, the very same people would cut me to the bone. As a multiyear survivor of extreme, multifaceted violence, I had every reason to be wary of Andres' tenderness. Yet, exploiting me was the furthest thing from his mind. He then started dropping by before dawn, regularly, sometimes unannounced to deliver my favorite breakfast combo from Jack in the Box. I knew he was harmless.

Andre was very frugal, in spite of his 100k salary which is public knowledge and listed on Payday California's website. He never gave me more than $40 bucks, even though I treated him like a King. But still, I knew he really liked me because his slithering tongue often tried to knock out my teeth as he tried to swallow my mouth and dislocate my jaw. He would hold me in his arms and silently gaze into my eyes causing me to jump up and wrap my long legs around his waist holding onto him as if he were my lifesaver.

While Andre waited to perform his heroic duties at the fire station, we would converse on the phone for hours regarding the rampant racism and discrimination, which plagued the LAFD, and how he often had to remind firefighters to be both compassionate and respectful of the poverty-stricken urban communities they were serving. All along he was crossing his fingers holding his breath hoping he would advance in the ranks.

I often *begged* him to let me visit the station to prepare one of my savory Turkey dinners for him and the other firefighters. He just chuckled at the notion. I even begged to do laundry but was never invited to perform any chores. I think there is a slight possibility he may have been embarrassed by me and wanted to keep our relationship a *secret*. Had he told me what Engine he was stationed at, I would have possibly made unwelcome stops. Our calls ended abruptly when he had flames to extinguish.

Andre was African American originally from the Northeast and had previously been employed as a meter maid. He *claimed* he was widowed. But once my antennas went up and my suspicions arose when I spotted Andre with a woman at an outdoor mall, The Grove, five minutes from my home. I felt like bum rushing him and locking lips while tackling him to the ground to score a touchdown. But I also felt that I didn't want him to get a glimpse of me, so I didn't do anything to bring attention my way. I just hid in plain view and watched them like a hawk, discreetly all the while wondering who the other woman was.

I texted him later and inquired who was the attractive lady. He informed me the woman was his sons'. He never referred to her as his wife or girlfriend. It wasn't my business and I left it alone out of respect for them. I was always drawn to fatherly figures as their nurturing attentive qualities turned me on.

I felt like I was sitting on top of the world when we ventured out on our first date to the cinema at the Grove. We viewed *Casino Royale* in the winter of 2006. Seated at the top row in the balcony section, we made out like two teenagers crawling into the threshold of puberty on their first date. I practically *melted* into his lap more than the butter melted into our mouths and bit his tongue off. I really didn't care what James Bond was accomplishing. Andre was my Bond.

I soon began monthly hormones and had them intramuscularly injected. I became more feminine in appearance and got more in touch with my feminine side. However, there was a hefty price to pay for injecting the monthly hormones, which were steroids, into my body. They began making extremely dramatic and *emotional* as if I was at an amusement park weekly on a roller coaster with broken brakes without a seatbelt. I allowed myself to open up and began longing for love and affection in ways like I had never before. I realized that Andre liked me no matter if I presented fully like a male or female. I didn't have to be glammed up like a Vogue cover girl for him to desire to spend quality time with me.

Around this time early one morning, Andre visited me.

"Hey baby".

As he stood in the doorway I was momentarily speechless and almost fell to my knees savoring viewing him wearing a button-downed bright yellow heavy jacket that exposed his semi hairy chest and carrying an ax. That almost sent me on a journey into deep space nine.

Anderson

"Ok," he said. "If you don't let me in, your neighbors are going to think there's a fire. So whats up?"

I wasn't used to men impressing me like this. He removed his gear and we laid up naked.

"I'm surprised you would allow yourself to get so heavily involved with someone like *me*," I said. "Considering the circumstances under which we met."

He remained silent. I think he was just as surprised. Through Andre, I discovered you never know where you can find companionship, a friend or love.

I knew I liked Andre because he represented to me what I desired in my life, a dominant, attentive, aggressive, affectionate responsible man. I really enjoyed seducing him and holding his attention. I believe what made Andre so vital to me at that time was the fact that he was able to answer lingering questions regarding something I along with my mother had been obsessing over. I had a sister Shayla. She was homeless. In February of 2005, she was residing in South Central Los Angeles on 60th and Western in a closed down furniture business building with other transients. They had been kicked out on numerous occasions but always managed to regain entry. During her last occupation of the building with several other people, it burned down completely. Shayla was the only one to perish and we had no corpse to grieve over.

So, after relaying the details to Andre, I quizzed him. "Do you think it was painful?"

Andre shook his head slightly grinning at me. "Wait a minute first you tell me Eddie visited your home after you put an ad in the LA Xpress using his mother's name Lillian, now this. Kina, sometimes I don't know what to believe with you."

Snapping my lips, frustrated and in defense mode, I responded, "I know the stories I am sharing with you read like fiction but they are all past real events. I know what day it is and I know who the sitting President is. Do you need to see her autopsy and fire incident report?"

With a look of seriousness, Andre responded, "More than likely the toxic smoke would have rendered her unconscious before the flames charred her. So, it's a high possibility that she didn't suffer."

"That's nice to know. There was only a tiny piece of her skin left on her body that made it easy for the coroner to identify her as black. She also had drugs in her system so I wondered if that played a role in any type of pain she may have felt."

Andre then placed his hand on my neck slightly massaging it and whispered, "I'm sorry that happened to your sister. I didn't mean to offend you."

I replied "I'm happy I finally have some closure. Thank you."

Nahshon Anderson is an award-winning artist from Altadena, California. They are a contributing writer in the anthology, Happy Hour: Our Lives in Gay Clubs and is working on memoir Shooting Range. www.nahshondionanderson.com.

The Guest
Annette Covrigaru

Her breathing slowed when the guest walked through the door, but her daughter didn't notice. The dusty sunrays flickered on the bedroom wall, then steadied their light, dim. It was nearing 3 o'clock and she could hear the cicadas in the garden, the cat skimming the couch, the front door opening, closing, opening. Muffled yet booming were these microscopic features of life, announcing themselves to her like a pestersome mosquito whose buzzing dominates all that is heard, and silences the rest.

The guest stood before her at the foot of the bed, gripping the wooden bedframe with one hand, patting the corner of the blanket with the other. She watched the guest's fingers slide along the covers, sinuous from the body beneath. *My body,* she thought. Indeed, it was her body. She felt her exhalations, parting sporadically from her lips. She could feel as they rippled down her breasts, through her torso, to her knees. She felt the inhalations cocooning in her abdomen, each one nestled on a rib like a poet on a hammock, swaying, thinking.

She was, herself, a poet – not by choice, of course (was there ever a choice for a poet?) but perhaps by coercion, some innate allure. It may have started at her family's ranch. The land was blotches of blue, hints of green, strokes of pale. She would follow streams for hours – because the land had hours to give, and hours to take – until she could not recognize where she was, or if this was the same ranch, and was this even the same stream I began with, or had it forked somewhere along the way? In the evenings she could hear the bison huffing and stomping behind the sound of her mother playing Joan Baez on guitar.

Nature was her mother tongue; she was fluent in river tides and bird whispers. At three years old, she stepped on a red anthill and her lower half was engulfed by stinging, burning. Her mother sprung into the house and ran cold sink-water over her legs and stomach. Later at night she would pick dead ants out of her bellybutton, drowned in a pool of her body. This, her first memory – the burn, the cold, and her mother's worried eyes.

Now her eyes were flittering, and in the brief slits of vision she saw her daughter wearing those same worried eyes. Hers were brown and bug-like, knowing and curious. Her eyes. They were young, they were sorrow, life seeing life burn out. And then a flash, or something like it, of her daughter's college graduation. Preparing for a photo, just the two of them, the daughter's head tilted up high in triumph, diploma in hand, and then kissing her cheek. The chilled pressure of her daughter's lips jolted her heart. In that moment, the cancer was gone.

And now her daughter kisses her cheek and rubs her scalp once more. The guest nods, motions with languid fingers like disentangled roots, and speaks, gently, as if the words are written on paper.

And yet, she hears herself.

All goes onward and outward, nothing collapses. And to die is different from what any one supposed, and luckier.

Annette Covrigaru is a queer American-Israeli writer based in Brooklyn, N.Y. They were a Lambda Literary Emerging LGBTQ Voices nonfiction fellow and writer-in-residence in 2014 and 2017, respectively. Their work has appeared in The Kaaterskill Basin Review, TQ Review and Stitch. They are the editor and creator of All Things Jesbian, an LGBTQIA Jew(ish) litzine (allthingsjesbian.com). Annette is currently completing a master's degree in Holocaust Studies through the University of Haifa.

acknowledgments

Very special thanks and appreciation to:

Rachel Linn for the cover art of this book,

Garth Greenwell for his powerful introduction,

Tony Valenzuela, William Johnson, Brandi M. Spaethe, and Kyle Sawyer of Lambda
Literary for their tireless work, dedication and vision,

and

Amazon.com for its support of Lambda Literary.

Cover illustration: Rachel Linn

Rachel Linn holds an MFA in creative writing from the University of Washington,
where she received the Eugene Van Buren Prize for her thesis project. Her writing
and illustrations have appeared or are forthcoming in Typehouse, Storm Cellar,
The Future Fire, and elsewhere.

To see more of Rachel's work please visit her website at rslinn.com.

Made in the USA
Middletown, DE
30 April 2021

38727070R00176